By the same author:

Human Energy Systems

Voluntary Controls

The Path of Action

IT'S NOT WHAT YOU EAT, BUT WHAT EATS YOU

IT'S NOT WHAT YOU EAT, BUT WHAT EATS YOU

by Jack Schwarz

CELESTIALARTS

Berkeley, California

The author and publisher make no medical claims, direct or implied, for anything mentioned in this book.

This book is presented here as a work of health education and cultural interest.

The reader should consult a licensed physician for any condition that logically requires their services. This book is not intended as a substitute for medical care.

CELESTIAL ARTS
P.O. Box 7327
Berkeley, California 94707

Cover design by Ken Scott
Text design by Paul Reed
Typography by HMS Typography, Inc.

Library of Congress Cataloging-in-Publication Data

Schwarz, Jack.
    It's not what you eat, but what eats you.

    1. Health.   2. Mind and body.   3. Vitality.
4. Nutrition   I. Title.
RA776.5.S33 1988   613.2   88–4331
ISBN 0–89087–527–8

First Printing, 1988

Manufactured in the United States of America

5   6   -   93

Contents

Acknowledgment

Special thank you's to Steve Guettermann for his excellent writing, editing and total support for this text. Thank you to Tom Luhnow for his creative ideas to get this book started and to my staff for their input and effort. To enthusiastic David Hinds, our publisher for his support.

A special thank you to my partner, Lois A. Scheller Schwarz for her visionary ideas, prompting and hours of constant work.

DEDICATED TO
THE HEALTH, HARMONY, AND PEACE
FOR
ALL BEINGNESS

Introduction

It's Not What You Eat, But What Eats You discusses a process of individual energy transformation for better health. What is health, what is diet, and what is nutrition? Better understanding of these processes allows transformations to occur in your life.

General nutritional needs throughout the stages of life, from prenatal to old age, are discussed, and how these needs are influenced by the physiological and mental changes taking place within you. This will help you to know how to maintain your integrity and excitement. I describe these processes of transformation and how to integrate your physical, mental, and emotional aspects into dynamic, healthful radiance. The end result is mind–body harmony, through which you can create a more unadulterated, undiluted life, a spiritual life.

Often within this book I use metaphors and analogies from many different disciplines; these should not be taken literally. This book is not meant to be scientific theory, but rather a summation of observations acquired during many years in a practice of counseling individuals. I hope that it will stimulate you to become more conscious of the mind–body relationship, and realize that food is not necessarily equivalent to nutrition.

1

An understanding of the mind–body process of energy transformation requires an understanding of the behavior and function of different qualities of energy and how they operate within the universe. The twofold nature of the universe mirrors the bipolar nature of the human mind–body. I discuss how this translates into the food we need to transform. We need to transform food and energy from the molecular state back to the ionic state and ultimately to radiant energy, which is the nascent state of the universe and ourselves.

Most people believe that we eat to get energy. We do not. We eat to activate energy, and many of our health and nutrition problems stem from the fact that we work with health, nutrition, and biochemistry almost totally on the molecular level. By holding onto the molecular form, the natural flow of energy and transformation through the mind and body become stagnated, and thereby the process of health becomes stagnated. When we hold onto form, energy becomes stagnated. Over time, stagnations manifest in the body as illness and disease.

Disease, or dis-ease, occurs when energy transformation, that is, cycles of creation and destruction, is not allowed to occur. Disease can also be part of the normal health transformation process as a person flows through changes of life and changes of consciousness. I categorize certain diseases which, if they are allowed to run their course and are understood, are part of healthful transformations. Disease can destroy a form of health which is no longer appropriate for a person. By applying principles of transformation, a person can discover how to enter a healthier state, the state of health needed for a new level of beingness.

In this book you learn how to adapt your body to new functions and opportunities represented by different stages of life and personal growth. Ideally, this information will lead you to understand others better, especially family members, and you can assist each other with change.

Adapting to changing functions relates back to nutrition. The body needs to be in a proper rhythm to transform the food ingested, or otherwise that food, no matter how high its quality, can become toxic to the body. I detail sources of toxins, including those derived from mental and emotional stagnations, how these toxins affect and are manifested in the body, and ways to eliminate the toxins while toning the body. This is followed by a discussion on how you can assess your health state and be sensitive to your body's language so that you can choose ways to detoxify, thus eliminating both the symptoms and causes of toxins and disease.

I discuss foods and biotonics as sources of necessary nutrients and electrical potentials to reinforce your understanding of the energy principles. I also talk about ways you can apply this understanding to your health and physical world.

Rapid social and environmental changes are affecting the evolution of our bodies. To maintain health we must keep pace with these changes. We must have a healthful rhythm between our inner environment, which comprises our bodies, minds, and emotions, and our outer environment. I discuss how human behavior has affected the outer environment. The energy force, which has been crucial in the evolution of our physical makeup, affects such things as the electromagnetic field of the Earth. There are ways to direct ourselves to a healthy involvement with the natural processes of creation and destruction. We do not need to be manipulated by self-inflicted ill health or panic over what may seem to be an increasingly hostile environment. We need to understand the properties of the Earth and sun, because their electrical potentials are in us. The main aim of all therapeutic methods, including nutrition, should be directed to restoring, preserving, and regenerating electrical potentials, because it is the electrical potential of the body which holds the key to the miracles and mysteries of health and healing.

Information on how energy becomes transformed in the body is included, but it is not my purpose to detail basic metabolism or give material which can be found elsewhere.

My hope is that this book will educate you to monitor the constant energy transformations occurring within your mind–body and the universe. Suggestions are given on how to function more fully and joyfully in a world you help create.

Chapter 1

It's Not What You Eat, But What Eats You

Tremendous social and environmental changes have paralleled the advancements and discoveries of technology.

We have effected change not only through the exploitation of natural resources, but also because social changes have occurred which are obscuring our understanding of the basic processes of life. Consequently, the Earth and the processes which give life to both the Earth and humanity have become more foreign to us and to our bodies. By viewing ourselves as separate from things which give life, we are actually affecting processes of energy exchange and evolution, which, until recently, were important aspects of our livelihood and survival.

For instance, the Earth does not look as it did six decades ago. We see a change in the substance of the Earth itself. The fire in the hollow Earth is more active. There is much greater movement there, because forces, especially electromagnetic forces, are being disrupted by artificial electromagnetism. This new electromagnetism has a much greater amplitude, or power, and a wider range of frequencies than the field in which life on Earth has evolved. Nuclear explosions and other disturbances in and beyond our atmosphere, as well as underground, have caused changes in the substances which sustain the Earth and changes in the energy field in which the Earth operates. Because we take these substances into our body through food and our interaction with the environment, it is important to understand these processes as they relate to health and well-being. It is also important to understand the processes which create, maintain, and restore both the environment of the Earth and the environment of the body. We and the Earth have evolved together. We have always affected one another, but the speed of our mutual change has never approached what we are now experiencing. If we understand the processes of change, we can better direct the energies which regulate our health. Health is a continuous, dynamic process of change. Your state of health is the state of your energy, as well as an application of your energy.

When humanity was of an agricultural world, we interacted with the Earth in a much more direct way. We did not have synthetic chemicals and fertilizers. Everything was done in a natural way, a way which was part of the processes of life and death or, in other words, transformation. Of course the death of one thing sustained the life of another, for in order to bring forth a new state or product, something needed to change form, that is, die. Problems would arise when things held on too long to a state and did not release that material, that energy, so that the processes could continue.

The most fertile soil was provided by the interaction between plants and animals. There was a continuous exchange. Cattle, for example, took in food, and then gave it back to the Earth as manure, as fertilizer. That fertilizer affected the chemistry of the soil in many ways. It not only was a direct source of nutrients for plants, but it caused micronutrients to be released from the minerals of the Earth, which were needed for the plants as well as the animals. This richness of the soil did not stay the same. For years this fertile state continued to improve, as these processes were allowed to occur. We partook in that process. We understood the universal law of continuous transformation, which says that whatever the body takes in, it puts out in a changed form, but that changed form becomes a nutrient for that which we will eventually take in again.

Today, we often have the misunderstanding that the food we eat, especially if it is pure and natural, will provide us with the nutrients we need. This is not necessarily so, because the human body has changed. The body is in conflict, struggling to adapt itself to radical changes of food and environment, even though it is still influenced by the processes which occurred for thousands of years, and were occurring up to sixty years ago. You can think of this conflict as cosmic jet lag.

Now, the human body has to adapt to substances that have been synthetically created. Their formula is the same as that of the natural foods, but lacks one thing—the intrinsic factor of life. Synthetics have very little charge, very little potential. As such, they cannot activate themselves to discharge energy. By mimicking natural substances with synthetics, we have, in a sense, been cloning. Cloning has not been very successful as of yet. We have been able to artificially create the *form* of some animals, and they were alive for some seconds, and then they died. The clones were charged, too, but the charge was of such a low power that the clones did not have the capacity to discharge energy sufficiently to resonate with the rest of life. There was not enough tension to transform that energy or to express that energy. It had no energy in motion, no E motion. The intrinsic factor to activate that vitality can take place only if there is an appropriate combination of positive and negative polarity-charged particles, which have enough power to continuously activate a state of transformation.

I will explain this concept of transformation by comparing the qualities of synthetics and natural substances.

In the process of transformation, elements go through different stages. In all living organisms the process of transformation takes place as an electrical activity. Within the universe, or the universal environment, elements are in their free state, or nascent state, which I call their radical free state. (Please do not confuse this term with *free radical*, which is a state of destruction to the normal processes of the body. The dictionary defines a free radical as something which goes through a reaction without being changed!) In this radical free state, elements represent electropotentials, meaning they have the potential to become part of the body's electrical life processes. Generally speaking, these potentials are either electrically positive, electrically negative, or neutral. A neutral has the ability to behave as a positive or a negative, depending upon what is needed for a specific function. This bipolar nature of positive and negative is witnessed universally in electricity and magnetism. We describe bipolar also as masculine–feminine, action–reaction, acid–alkaline, contracting–expanding, and many other ways.

This electropotential is what gives natural substances their energy content, their charge. Between these particles there is a continuous process of charge and discharge occurring. The positive is a condensing form of energy. It provides form. Most foods, even acid foods, have a predominantly positive charge. The positive helps maintain the body's form. The negative is an expanding form of energy. The negative releases material out of form.

Positively and negatively charged particles are continuously involved in the bipolar process of transformation. Remember, no matter what you put into your body, it has to change. It is the *change* that makes the activity. It is the charge that gives you vitality, not the substance itself. In other words, we do not eat to *get* energy; we eat to *activate* energy.

The difference between the seemingly lifeless synthetics and the living organics and inorganics is a difference in the energy content of the molecules. The electropotential of living organisms is continuously active. Living organisms generate and regenerate and that, again, is the intrinsic factor of life. In a synthetic formula which follows the exact chemical formula of a natural substance, molecules are formed, but there is no transformation. There is no discharge, no breaking down, because there is not much charge to begin with. Synthetics can transform only when brought into contact with substances which already have the capacity to transform. Those substances can act upon that synthetic and induce it out of its molecular form. Later we will discuss the direction-giving aspects of these energies, which we call mind, and relate that to the mind–body interaction of health.

Most synthetic chemicals are derived from formulas which use carbon extracted from crude oil. Oil is of the earth. It is part of the living process of continuous change of the earth. There are living characteristics in the oil as long as it is in the ground. But when we take oil from the ground and start to break it down to create synthetics, that original substance is not an organism anymore.

The difference between synthetics and natural substances is like the difference between drawing a house and building a house. It takes a certain amount of energy to build a house. It also takes a certain amount of energy to draw a house, but you could not compare that energy to people walking around carrying bricks, putting up walls, and nailing down a roof. There is something missing: the life process. It is the same with synthetics. Each element in a synthetic does have a charge, but it is of a lower potential because it is molecular. The synthetic does contain a certain energy, but the dynamics of generation are not present. There is so little charge in synthetics that they take forever to rot, and rotting is a process of life too.

If you take a substance out of, for example, a plant, the substance retains the capacity for self-transformation and regeneration. This capacity is not found in a test tube formula. Synthetic materials can transform themselves only by being brought into contact with other substances that self-transform. That process of a natural substance activating a synthetic to transform itself is a mechanical dynamics rather than a life dynamics. This means the body has to work harder to get value from synthetic foods and medicines. It has to boost them into activity. If the body is already lacking vitality, it may not be able to provide that boost, and substances which normally would help us, or at least not hurt us, become toxic.

Let us take one other example. I can walk and use my own electrical potential energies. Or I can sit in a car and be driven, but that way I am moved by the car rather than moving myself. Now, why am I able to move myself? Because the life-intrinsic factor is there. It is only when that life-intrinsic factor does not work anymore that I *have* to be driven by a car. If this were not true, I could walk to my own funeral! But I would not because when that life-intrinsic factor is withdrawn, the life process does not get mental direction any longer, and those dynamics which are present when the electrical potentials of the mind direct it are gone. When that direction-giving aspect is withdrawn, there is a process of decay, which is a process of energy, too. Decay is a process of discharge, but it is a lesser voltage than that given off when the person was alive, because nothing is regenerated anymore. It is transformed to its original substance again—ash. All the life is eventually released out of it. Ash has absolutely no measurable voltage. Without the life-intrinsic factor that material is no longer directed by the law of transformation. Not until that ash totally breaks down and releases, or discharges, all its stored electropotential, will it be *recycled* and reformed into a life force which has the ability to generate and regenerate. A natural substance can get to the ash state relatively quickly, but ash itself takes years to break down because, like the synthetics, it has practically no charge. Thus the materials of which synthetics are created can be thought of as a kind of ash.

What makes defining the processes, qualities, and states of energy difficult is that they are inseparable from one another. Also, in defining them, we are attempting to hold them in order to identify them. But because they are in a continuous state of exchange, it is important to realize that though we may speak of the mind, or of the body, or of molecules, or of electropotentials, or of thoughts, their dynamics mean their effects upon energy and matter are not limited to just the state in which they occur. So we are not only responsible for our body or for our health. We are responsible for the whole universe. And the universe is responsible for us!

The mind is represented as electropotentials. Thoughts outside the body are a formation of electropotentials. Both the mind and thoughts outside the body can be described as particles of energy with a certain frequency and a certain amplitude. The brain processes information of the mind. Through the brain the mind directs the dynamics of the body. Every food particle, every nutrient within the Earth, can be found in our outer environment as an electropotential capable of entering into the electrochemical processes of the body, at which time it can be identified as a specific element. Our thoughts are created from very similar particles as those in the food we eat, but the particles are in different combinations. The combinations, based upon their function, form a specific state and quality of energy. The mind, then, has the same nutrients as we find in the body, only we find them as pure nutrients, as electroactive particles, in the mind. The moment they enter our body by the *form* we have given them, they become active particles in the body and need to continue to be part of the continuous process of transformation. It is as Dr. Elmer Green stated in *Beyond Biofeedback*: "Every change in the physiological state is accompanied by appropriate change in the mental-emotional state."

I have often said all of the body is in the mind, but not all of the mind is in the body. That statement is not just philosophical. It has practical value! It is important to know what your food and nutritional needs are. It is just as important to know what your mental and emotional needs are and what the mind brings into the body. If you do not activate and express those particles which your mind has drawn out of the environment and brought into your body, they will become detrimental to your mental as well as physical health. Certainly your energy in motion will stagnate. Later we will discuss how thoughts become body chemistry.

Many people still feel their health is a specific form, a specific state, which is static. They have been taught that the body strives for homeostasis, which means "steady state." They think, Once I am healthy, I have my health, and that's that. But that is *not* the way it is. Health is a continuous, dynamic process of evolution to enhance your transformation—physical, mental, emotional, and spiritual. And what does the word *spiritual* mean? It is the totality of all processes, blending in a harmonious, universal rhythm. Spirit is pure, undiluted, unadulterated energy. At times it is ready to go into a process of dilution and adulteration to transform and to maintain the motion, the energy in motion, of the universe. We can also say that all matter is spirit, but not all spirit is matter. What we do not recognize to be spirit is that which is diluted and adulterated. It is our function through our physical, mental, and emotional activities and creativities to restore it to its original undiluted, unadulterated form.

We cannot see the mind, body, emotions, and spirit as separate from one another. They are all enhanced within one another. They need to interact. Mind, body, emotion, and spirit are merely labels for different qualities of energy. Through labeling we tend to identify with only the form we have labeled. We neglect the rest of the energies which are enhanced within that particular one and need to be released. Nourishing is an act of transformation. It involves the body, the mind, and the energy in motion. That interaction affects the level of spirituality upon which we exist.

So I ask, Have you taken your food and made spirit out of it again? If you say yes, but you look dull, make sure that there are no pieces of food stuck between your teeth which have not become spirit—yet.

Many people have forgotten that the body is really the Earth. All the particles you can find in the universe you can find as particles on Earth. Consequently, every particle you can find in the Earth you can find in your body, if you maintain it. You can think of your body as being made up of three types of particles: mineral, plant, and animal. All particles found in each of these worlds can be found in your body, even though you would not find them as a mineral, or as a plant, or as an animal. If these particles were minerals, plants, or animals, we would not be human beings! This brings us again to the concept of health being both a form of energy and an application of energy. Our body form is a part of an evolutionary transformation state of all the body particles. This makes us responsible for the transformation of ourselves as well as those particles of the body. This might sound like a burden, but this dimension of our beingness allows us to function much more fully and joyfully in this environment than if we did not share this bond with that which sustains us. Isolation, not involvement, is the real burden. And, if we had never had a transforming mental state, we would still be a little piece of coal in the ground trying to become a diamond.

If we look deeply into the form our body's cells have taken, we see a primitiveness in the cells and the structures within them. They mirror how the Earth was formed and crystallized through the exchanges of fire, air, and water. Our protoplasm, the main substance of which our body is made, is a continuously changing, gelatinlike substance science calls crystalo-colloidal, which means it is crystal. We are crystal-operating individuals.

We know crystals are in radios, televisions, and computers, but why do we find a continuous process of crystallization taking place in the body? What is so special about crystal? Communication! Crystals refract light. They receive and transmit impulses. So it should not surprise us that if crystallization does not take place in the body in an appropriate way, the mind and the body will not be able to communicate with each other! A crystal-clear body supplies the mind with the instrument to communicate with its environment in the highest ways.

It is fascinating to realize that the healthier a person becomes, and the more involved with life that person is, the less food he or she eats. We often comment how radiant that person is. We notice how energetic and how charged that person is. That person is charged because he or she is in a continuous state of discharge, of generation and regeneration. This state involves the same electrical processes of electropotentials, which form and maintain the Earth. The Earth gets nourished directly from electropotentials. The radiant person does too.

If you impair your mind's influence upon your body by not allowing your mind to spontaneously partake in the process of nourishing your body, stagnation takes place. The food you eat stagnates, because you are not expressing all your nutrients. You see, the food you eat is part of your energy in motion too, and if you force that E motion to stagnate, your mind will stagnate. You will lose your dynamism. If you force your emotions to stagnate, you impair your discharge, your expression, your *radiance*. With all the things we take in from our environment, we must remember to express them appropriately. Appropriate expression generates and maintains the flow of energy, in all its forms, through you. Expression is a nutrient too.

In the following chapters I hope to show how these processes of transformation are manifested in the mind and body, and discuss ways in which you first can observe these life processes functioning within you and then can direct changes to occur which enhance your unique expression of energy—your health.

Chapter 2

Food for Thought, Food for Body

As individuals, our consciousness is a component of universal energy. This universal energy differs in quality according to the environment in which it is found, because each type of energy must adapt itself in order to exist in any environment. This energy can be considered to be in the form of particles. Each particle within a specific environment is unique, but will have qualities similar to all other particles within that environment. For example, light represents a specific state of energy, with similar particles of light existing in specific parts of the light spectrum. These particles have a certain kind of energy. We see light which exists at 350 cycles per second as green. Light particles which exist at 260 cycles per second are red. In short, each color and hue, which are qualities of energy, can be predictably found at specific wavelengths.

Electrical energy is another example. Electrical energy is generated by friction, induction, or chemical changes of proton, neutron, and electron particles. These changes can be perceived and measured as magnetic, chemical, or radiant (or any combination of these), and are properties of *all matter, including the human body.*

Not only are the body's cells adapted to charge, store, and discharge electricity, but the protoplasm within the cells of all living organisms operate on the same bipolar principles. We can further verify the fact that the body can charge, store, and discharge electrical energy by observing that engineers are making prototypes of computer microchips made of enzymes derived from plant and animal substances. Why would they want to use enzymes instead of silicon chips? Because in addition to their electrical properties, enzymes are capable of self-repair, even when taken out of their natural state. These enzymes are being used in computers as replacements for microchips, which supports the fact that living matter has the capacity to accumulate electropotentials, which are like a memory. The memory in silicon chips is nothing more than electropotentials. There are no words, numbers, or images there, but electrical vibrations and patterns, which form words, numbers, and images, much like what happens in the brain.

The energy patterns which we perceive and identify as words, numbers, and images consist of fast-moving electropotentials. They have the capacity to create a certain form for a certain moment, and then almost instantaneously continue with their process of transformation. Silicon itself is important to the body. It exists as a vital component of a variety of crystals which radiate energy and nerve impulses, as well as assist with healing. Silicon is the most abundant chemical element found in nature, with the exception of oxygen, with which silicon combines to form silica (SiO^4), a crystal substance.

In order for health and nutrition to be understood, we must understand the processes of energy which affect the human mind–body, or the human energy system. You, as a unique expression of your universal energy, are in a constant state of transformation. By understanding your uniqueness and the processes which maintain you, you can better understand how you affect the outer environment, your personal environment, and your health, and how that with which you interact affects you. You are unique because each particle of which you are composed is unique as is each particle of universal energy. All particles are similar, but no two are the same.

The energy and properties of the Earth environment give the group of particles of each person its capacity to direct itself to human energy and to maintain its uniqueness, because it has individualized itself in this environment. And, as no one can have the same particles as anyone else, or occupy the same space, that group has to adapt to that specific environment. Your group of human energies includes your mind as well as your body. The mind is the energy which, through the brain, directs the body. Any act is unique. This relates to the nourishment you require in order to function as a healthy individual capable of pursuing your unique purposes.

The mental environment is much different from the physical environment. The processes which affect these particles of energy outside the body operate in a totally different way from those which affect the particles of energy inside the body. The mental processes affect the energy potentials of these particles. That is, the particles adapt themselves to the mental environment. These particles have a certain consciousness and certain potentials in order to function there, in order to know themselves and that environment. That is the purpose of transformation. For every process, a particle or a group of particles is involved in moving from environment to environment. The nature of the environment determines which particle potentials, or electropotentials, are released. Because the environment is continuously transforming itself too, we never know in advance what potential needs to be activated and expressed. This brings us again to the point that we eat to activate energy rather than to get energy, so we must be willing to change our diet as we change.

We are members of many environments simultaneously. These include our world, work, home, and personal environments, as well as our mental and emotional environments. Health problems may occur when we fail to appropriately transform and express what we consciously and unconsciously take in from our environmental interactions. For example, emotional energy and physical energy can both significantly influence your health, but emotional strength and physical strength are two very different qualities of energy. The ways in which each person experiences and uses these energies help to define his or her uniqueness. The experience and use of emotional and physical strength affect our integration with everything in which we are involved as well as how we perceive ourselves. We must look at the different aspects of ourselves and our environments as energy, because that is really all there is. When we have mastered our understanding of the processes of energy, we will be much less offended by anything the environment may offer us. We can then commit ourselves to fully and joyfully expressing ourselves, and we can fearlessly interact with our environments. We become warriors rather than worriers. The more environments in which we knowingly operate, the more of our potentials we express, and the fewer stagnations we will have.

It is the same with the universe as with the human body. Depending upon where that energy in motion directs itself and in what kind of environment it occurs, it will have a different state of transformation and different energy potential. In order to function in a particular environment, consciousness, which I use as another word for energy, needs to have the potential to function in that environment. A person's potential is like a toolbox. The environment in which that person finds himself or herself determines which tools he or she will use in order to best function there. If that person is in the woods, he or she may frequently use an ax. If that person is later in an office, he or she may put away the ax and do some work with a computer. That does not mean the ax is nonfunctional. It just means the person has put it back in the toolbox because he or she has chosen not to use the ax in an office environment.

Truly we are often unaware of our potentials, because we try so hard to maintain our environment, to keep everything as it is, so we do not have to change. In that way we keep ourselves from knowing our uniqueness and totality. But a person's uniqueness constantly transforms itself, because the environment constantly transforms itself. We can compare ourselves to drops of water in an ocean. A drop of water is really very much aware of being a drop, and it knows it is somewhere in a wave, but it is so busy with its dropness that it does not pay attention to its total environment and its total self, which might be, for example, the Pacific Ocean. But as the ocean changes, the wave changes, and as the wave changes, the drop changes, for whatever purpose the wave needs. So the drop and the ocean affect one another.

Our inability to transform everything we take into our mind–body not only creates health problems, but also determines some of our nutritional needs. When we stagnate, the world around us continues to change, so our environmental relationships also change. Rather than being in rhythm with our environment we are lagging behind in the process of expression. The body through the mind knows that. So the body says, Okay, I have to accelerate, but I cannot accelerate unless I get a little more gas. I better eat some food. What part of me has become stagnant and needs to be reactivated? We need to become aware of what it is we are not expressing in order to know what we need. As with everything in the universe, expression is a bipolar process. You take in something, transform it, and give it back. We will discuss this further when we talk about maladies which arise in the body as symptoms of stagnation.

Any denial of activity will hamper the electrical energy available for you to be healthy. No involvement, no evolvement; it is that simple. If we feel we are evolving too slowly, we should figure out how much time we spend in a day trying to avoid involvement. This represents locked-up energy. If we pile more food on top of that locked-up energy, expecting that food to activate us, all we are going to do is add to that lack of involvement, because the food will become poison to our body. We will not break the food down by active involvement. This is why health professionals say, "Please exercise." Get that body moving. That way you help your physical–chemical situation. Even if you get no joy out of the exercise, at least you will have a better metabolism, a better assimilation of food, and a better oxygenation of your body.

Spontaneous expression of your energy potentials is the best method of nourishment and the best way to maintain your health. This spontaneous expression involves a total commitment from your body, mind, emotions, and spirit to your actions, without concern for the result of that activity. I call this total, unconditional commitment excitement!

Expression is an electrical activity. The electropotentials of the body and the electropotentials of the body's cells keep the body's activities going. This is not hard to understand when we read off a list of certain elements the body needs, such as zinc, copper, and iron, which, ideally, nicely function in the dielectric saline water solution of our body. Our bodies are wet batteries! Every cell is like a minibattery, with each holding positive and negative charges. The magnetic part of the body's energy field can be described as the monitoring part, which maintains a rhythmic balance. Electrical energy conditions the body to manifest a quality of vitality, or life.

Let me explain what I mean by the preceding sentence. I could, for example, say that I am alive but that the table I write upon is dead. But the table is alive, too; it simply is not as vital as I am. That is one of the reasons I am not the table and the table is not me. The table is as vital as it needs to be in its state of tableness. We need to see life in everything and measure everything's vitality by its function. It is painful to observe people who have all the vitality of a table. I have never yet seen a table with the vitality of a human being! If you go to the doctor when you are feeling low, the doctor will examine you and tell you that you have become very tablelike. She will, of course, use a different term. She will tell you that you have a low level of resistance. What is she measuring? She is measuring the voltage which radiates from you, which emanates the activity and the inactivity of the nutrients in your body. The nutrients are particles with electropotentials, which give that vitality its quality, be it high or low. Your vitality lies in the principles of bipolarity and the dynamics of bipolar particles. Each cell in your body has charges: electropositive and electronegative. We could call the charges masculine and feminine. Or, if you have studied Asian medicine, you might say yang and yin. Electrically oriented people might call them cations and anions, which are positive and negative ions.

Today, with our tendency to go overboard on everything that seems to be "good for you," we find people believing that negative air ions are better than positive air ions. That is not so at all. We need a predominance of positive air ions in relation to negative air ions. Currently, however, there is an *excess* of positive air ions in our body and in our environment. Why? Because we want to maintain the form of everything. We are afraid we might not recognize the next form. So we become mentally constipated. We become obese. We are afraid the new form might be different from that with which we are familiar. If there is change we ask, Now what do I do? The positive is not better than the negative, nor is the negative better than the positive. They merely have different functions.

To explain what these positive and negative charges do, let me ask you, When you go to the store, what kind of battery do you buy? You buy an alkaline battery, which has a predominantly positive charge. When the battery gets too much acid, what happens? It leaks! It deteriorates! Because every cell in your body carries two charges, you can say every cell both receives and transmits. The positive charge contracts and condenses. It receives. It creates form. The negative charge releases and carries material away. The positive charge is at the center of the cell and the negative charge is at the outside of the cell. To continue to live and maintain vitality, these two charges must be in comparative balance. I say comparative balance because a vital principle is overlooked when we try to get in balance. Being in balance is a state of health, but it is not a healthy state.

For example, take a scale, which is also called a balance. The balance has a fulcrum in the middle, with a basket of equal weight on each end. That is a beautiful balance, isn't it? The baskets are motionless at the point of the fulcrum. Once it reaches a balance, what happens to the scale? It stops. It is static. And what else has been reached besides a balance? Death. Death has been reached because the activity has been taken away. There is no change any longer. The baskets no longer affect one another. They are in perfect balance. That is why I say comparative balance, because comparative balance does not mean that every particle of potassium in your body has a particle of sodium. Comparative balance means your ions are functional, with no deficiency and no excess. There is activity and communication between them.

A confusion between being in balance and being functional is often encountered in medical centers. Let us say a person is found to be deficient in functional potassium. The laboratory may interpret this to mean the person has excessive sodium. Potassium and sodium are two substances found in different areas of nerve cells. So what happens? We try to restore that person's balance by taking out what is thought to be excessive sodium. We take enough sodium out of the basket so the middle of the balance comes to rest upon the fulcrum and that person is now in balance. How marvelous. But what state has been created? We started with a state of too little functional potassium and replaced it with a state of too little functional sodium. In this case the task should not have been to remove the sodium, but rather to activate the potassium, so it was in comparative balance with the sodium, for optimal functioning of the nerves.

When we assess people at the Aletheia H.E.A.R.T. Center, we advise them on nutrition and diet in order to attain and maintain that comparative alkaline–acid balance. Many of these people are not only toxic, but their toxic state is highly acidic. No wonder they are fatigued and diseased! No wonder they say someone has pulled their cork! When I perceive their energy field, it indeed feels as if energy is leaking out of it. Their process of transformation is not happening in the appropriate way. They are destroying their structure rather than transforming it; cellular suicide rather than cellular rejuvenation is taking place.

The predominance of a positive charge means abundant energy, vitality, and endurance; and quick generation and regeneration of structure. If you want to achieve and maintain a comparatively balanced state, you will have an assorted diet, which helps you maintain a slightly predominantly alkaline state. That is one of the generalities we *can* make about diet, because if you are acid you will not feel strong. You will not say, Wow! I am ready to go! You will say, Can I wait a little while? I need to charge first.

Comparative balance is absolutely essential if we are to maintain the processes of activity which change energy into forms and forms into energy. Those are the body's processes. If you have an absolute balance, you take away the vitality, because you take away the activity.

Rather than trying to understand the processes of life and trying to understand why they function as they do, we often choose to interfere. We take nutrients out of our body as we take nutrients out of our foods. Cholesterol, for example, is vital for body maintenance. Our brain has a tremendous need for it, as does our skin and many of our tissues. But it has been identified as a culprit in heart attack victims, so we say, I must cut back on my cholesterol. No more fats. No more eggs. Science might go a step further and say, Aha, let us create an egg without cholesterol. But if we were to take the cholesterol out, the egg would cease to be an egg, because we would have interfered with its life processes. If we have a problem with the cholesterol in eggs, we should reduce our intake of them, not change them for our sake. We know too little of the processes of life in that egg, not to mention too little about our own life processes, to begin interfering with them. We must adapt ourselves to what we find within food and not make it toxic by taking out something or putting in something. Toxicity results from altering the comparatively balanced ionic state of foods.

In the cell, predominance of the negative charge will tend to fatigue it. The cell will be discharging to an excessive degree. Many people are fatigued. That is because they have a predominantly negative charge in their systems. There is an insufficient amount of appropriate activity happening in their bodies. There is an activity happening, but it is an activity of deterioration. They have either too much mental activity going on, and not enough physical activity, or too much physical activity going on and not enough mental activity. Life processes have become stagnated because there is separation rather than harmony between the mind and body.

In the classes and assessments we conduct at the Aletheia H.E.A.R.T. Center, we often speak of a person's radiance. What is this radiance, this light, of which we speak? It's a certain glow on a person's face or a particular sparkle in a person's eyes when he or she is truly involved and excited. From where does this light come? Well, the fact is that not only is your body a state of energy, but because of its electromagnetic properties, your body is the core of an electromagnetic energy field around itself. The field is actually part of you. This brings me again to the statement I am fond of making: *All of my body is in my mind, but not all of my mind is in my body.*

This energy field has seven discernable layers, or spheres, which, to an extent, represent such things as your physical, mental, and emotional states of health. I have treated the energy fields in detail in my book entitled *Human Energy Systems*, but I will give some additional information here to help you better understand your processes of health and radiance. Your radiance represents the quality of the energy field which surrounds you. This energy field is no esoteric or mystical idea that only very spiritual people have or can see. No, we all have fields through which we relate to our environments—our physical, mental, emotional, spiritual, interpersonal, and universal environments. Our energy fields are affected by and, in turn, affect the total state of health of our minds and bodies.

Through technology, medical science is becoming increasingly adept at measuring and giving diagnoses based upon the state of a person's energy field, as well as on the state of the individual energy fields of internal organs. The color, frequency, amplitude, and voltage of the electromagnetic field around the body is due to the type of radiant energy emitted from the electrochemical and biochemical actions occurring in the body. Observation of the energy field provides immediate information on the state of transformations which constantly occur within the mind and body. The task is to properly interpret that information. The layers closest to the body have electromagnetic properties which are similar to the properties of the body. The familiarity of these properties enable us to more readily perceive them, either directly through our senses or with the help of instruments. The farther from the human body we go, the more subtle the field becomes. But instruments can measure this field and, with proper training, people can begin to perceive aspects of it.

Though trained observers see the human energy field as light, it is light which is outside the spectrum of what is known as visible light. But most of us have eyes that are underused and underdeveloped. We use only about 10 percent of the available rods and cones of our retinas. In addition, the mechanisms in our brains which control vision are also underused and underdeveloped. Certain organs which enable us to see beyond the so-called visible spectrum need to be exercised and brought back into action, so we can enjoy the full benefits of our vision. This will help us with self-diagnosis and allow us to develop a clearer understanding of human energies. It will also provide a way to get immediate information on how our health is influenced by all our environments. *Human Energy Systems* gives exercises to improve vision and strengthen the eyes to aid in the perception of energy fields.

Radiance is emitted by activity—the activity of the mind, the body, nutrients, expressions, emotions—all the energies in motion. Full involvement of the body, mind, heart, and soul, without concern for the outcome of the activity, brings the processes of transformation to their most radiant state. Einstein once said, "The more momentum radiant energy has, the more time slows down for it." In other words, the more stagnant the energy, the less radiant it is. Or, to use an old proverb: Stagnant pools become cesspools.

Physicists have confirmed that lower energy fields cannot penetrate higher energy fields. This fact applies to our health. The more our energy is moving, the more power it has, and the greater our radiance. That is why we need activity—spontaneous, free-flowing activity.

Recall the statement I made a few pages ago that when you go to the doctor when you feel low, she will say that your resistance is low. It is the same as saying your radiance is low. When your resistance is low, you are much more prone to picking up things from your environment—things from people, things from the air, things from your mental stagnations. When I feel low I do not slow down further. I do not stay in bed and stagnate. I accelerate. I plunge myself into activity, body, mind, and soul. Time slows down for me, so I find it easier to find the time to do what I want. When you are fully involved with something, you may look at the clock and say, Wow, a whole hour went by! It felt like only five minutes. And for you, that is all that has happened. You have slowed down your aging process by speeding up your activities.

When you are fully involved, you are not at work. You are expressing. On the other hand, when you hate what you do and drag yourself through it, each minute feels like an hour. Imagine what you are doing to your body. You are getting old before you know it! In that state you can fall prey to any irritants which occur. You feel no joy in your expression. You can't get moving. You might go home, eat something, and flop in front of the television. That meal sits in your stomach as you lie on the couch. You feel dense, molecular. That food can only be activated by your physical, mental, and emotional activities and creativities. Your body must be active enough to break down that molecular food and remake it into what your body needs in order for your body to maintain itself, as well as express itself.

The single most important factor which affects your biochemical actions is the condition of the water in your body. It is the catalyst for chemical actions. When this salt water is in comparative balance, it does not conduct an electrical charge, as does impure water or unbalanced water. The water of your body insulates. It is dielectric. It allows the chemical actions to occur which activate the energy of your food and nutrients. When that body water is unbalanced, which means there is too much of this or too little of that, the electrical charges of those activities, if they occur at all, are not directed along the proper physiological pathways. That water no longer insulates. It has become conductive, and your energy leaks away. If your body is leaking energy, it cannot sufficiently charge and store the energy needed to transform what you eat and what you experience.

Resonance and Excitement

Resonance is the paramagnetic principle of like attracts like. This means that particles of a like charge, voltage, frequency, or amplitude attract and can transform themselves with one another. Magnetism affects denser forms in which opposites attract. It predominates in the layers closest to the body. Resonance predominates in the more subtle layers of the energy field, but it also affects the subtle energies which permeate the entire energy field. If the body is in a state where it is expressing and transforming much of what it takes in, then the radiant energy produced by that body will resonate with like particles in the environment. When this happens, all layers of the energy field become more subtle. The end result is that the more subtle particles of the energy field attract the more subtle particles of the environment. These new particles are conditioned by the energy field to the extent that the particles predominantly become more magnetic and less electric as they get closer to the body. This change happens because as the particles pass through the layers of the energy field they move through different environments and must adapt to each environment in order to function there.

The particles transform themselves until they reach an electromagnetic form in which they can be directed, assimilated, and used by the body. Then they go through the same electrochemical, biochemical, and molecular processes as would particles taken in through food. The molecules and ions enter into the body's metabolic processes and are attracted by tissues and organs which need their specific potential in order to function. As these processes activate additional energy, the body continues to emit its radiance, through which the physiological processes of transformation are nourished, so there is less need for food.

The physiological processes are identical, including forming the waste products of metabolism. I call this getting nutrients from the wholesaler rather than the retailer. This is why people who are excited and involved can do with less food and can eventually do without food. They get nourishment from their radiance and from the exchange of all these ingredients through subtle electromagnetic states into which they have brought themselves, yet they may excrete more waste than people who eat three times a day. The reason these people have more waste is that they have more activity going on. They essentially must excrete the ashes of their metabolic activity. Their body has more radiant activity, because it is not burdened with such things as trying to extract from a fast food hamburger whatever small amounts of nutrients it possesses.

Let me explain this with an analogy. Let us say I throw twenty logs into the fire. Some of the wood is dry oak, but most of it is wet and green birch, willow, and aspen. The wet, green logs of birch, willow, and aspen are going to impair the total heat of the fire if I do not have enough dry oak to overpower them. If there are any green logs I will not have a hot fire. I will have not only ashes from that fire, but also big chunks of stuff which did not metabolize. The dry oak, which represents pure energy, will burn hotter and faster. Over a period of time you will have more ashes from a hot fire than from a cool fire, and you will also get much more use from that hotter fire.

Every particle of food you take in must be remade before your body can use it. For example, if we take in starches, proteins, and fats, we must remake them into human starches, proteins, and fats, then break them down to activate energy. When you live with excitement, however, you reverse that process. You make starches, fats, and proteins from pure energy and allow those particles to partake in your processes without your body having to transform the voltage, frequency, and amplitude of those particles in order to make them usable.

Of course, all this is a fairy tale to most people, because science is not yet ready to accept that it is possible to obtain nourishment through resonance. I feel this concept will gain acceptance, though, as we learn more about the electrical and electromagnetic properties of human energies, as well as of the Earth and the universe. Some medical sciences, however, are beginning to change. For instance, electronic therapies which stimulate the body to heal itself are now being employed where surgery was once used. In these cases, instruments measure the electrical frequency and amplitude of a diseased tissue or organ to determine any deficiency or excess, which are always present simultaneously. Then electrical energy is directed to that area to restore its comparative balance again, to aid the body to attain and maintain its rhythm.

Endocrinologists these days are becoming neurophysiologists. They recognize the body is in an electrical state; this has been confirmed through studies upon the nature of the information given to the body via the nervous system. That information is electrical. So endocrinologists do not work just with the chemistry of hormones anymore. Endocrinology is now based upon the neurons, which are the activators of the electricity of the body and keep the body going. As we have become aware that each neuron is a radiant transmitter and receiver, so soon we shall realize that every particle of the body is a transmitter and receiver. The body also has *neuroinhibitors*, which means "regulators." Neuroinhibitors regulate what activities the body will be receptive to, how the body will respond, and when the response will stop.

Whether we are in a high radiant state, where the energy which emits from the body has a low frequency and high amplitude, or in a low energy state, where the radiant energy is of a high frequency and low amplitude, we still attract like particles from the environment. When you are not radiant because you are not active, you will attract low oscillatory vibrations. Everything we need to get from the outside comes in as energy. That energy has a certain vibratory rate. If you have energy which you have been holding onto for a long time, such as thoughts, desires, potentials, or nutrients, the vibration of that energy is very low. The energy is highly molecular. Your metabolism, therefore, is very slow. Your glands respond ever more slowly, because they are not being stimulated. The result is that you begin sponging in denser and denser materials. You become more susceptible to the effects of germs, bacteria, infection, negative thought patterns, and even heavy foods.

When these materials enter your body, they add to your low vibratory molecular structure. More molecules are formed and their energy, which you need to express, is stored as fatty acids and fatty oils, rather than carbohydrates and sugars, which your body breaks down to activate energy. The fats remain as fat, because your body does not have enough activity going on to convert them into carbohydrates and sugars. Because these fats are not releasing their sugars, you start to eat anything under the sun with sugar in it. This gives you a little pep in the short run, but adds more misery to your body in the long run because your warehouse is already loaded. You are not using what you have. The organs which are supposed to help transform fats to sugars become more dysfunctional, because they are not allowed to be active. This situation relates particularly to the thyroid, which works the general metabolism; the pancreas, which works with sugars; and the liver, which filters out toxins from the body. In order to change to a higher resistance level, or a higher radiance, the dense materials must be carried away. Yet they cannot be carried away if the organs are not functioning, because your body does not have the capacity to transform what needs to be transformed. That is why you need a transforming mental state too. There is no better way to metabolize than to always be excited and to express everything you absorb.

Remember, we are crystal-operating creatures. Our protoplasm is the main conduit of radiance and electricity through our body. *Protoplasm*, which means "first form," is a gelatinlike, 100 percent protein, crystalo-colloidal substance. These crystals are made largely from carbohydrates, which are specific combinations of carbon, hydrogen, and oxygen. These countless small, fine crystals of carbon conduct radiance and electrical impulses throughout your body.

The activity of the body's tissue salts, which I will work with in detail later, maintains the comparative balance of chemical activity in the body. The salts are a compound of two or more elements; usually one has a negative charge, and one has a positive charge. Tissue salts maintain the body's dielectric water, which provides the environment for other biochemical reactions. Tissue salts integrate and transform the radiant energy into a crystalo-colloidal form. The ions of dissolved salts regulate the chemical balance of protoplasm. The crystalo-colloidal protoplasm refracts the body's radiant energy, constantly separating out the potential qualities inherent in the energy in order to make it available to the body. What all this means is that the body, which is a crystal-operating system, responds to and with electrical impulses, allowing it to have very fast communication with itself. This is why and how the slightest alteration in the relative concentration of the salts will be registered by the organism and cause major and minor electromagnetic disturbances. These disturbances are specific to the affected tissue and specific to the elements involved in the disturbance. Consequently, though you may not be able to determine what and where an imbalance lies, the body is fully aware of it. The body will signal you with symptoms in order to get your attention. The symptoms are not the body trying to tell itself that something is wrong. It already knows what is wrong! The symptoms are there to get you to make changes in your body, mind, way of life, or outer environment.

For example, a person might be diagnosed as having too much stress in his life. His doctor may tell him he has to relax. Fine. I am all for relaxing, but I am not necessarily for reducing stress. Stress, after all, is an engineering term which simply means change. If you reduce the amount of stress to which you are subjected, you may be reducing your state of health and radiance. If we tell ourselves, I can't take that, we may live in fear, which can be just as damaging as stress. We can grow beyond stagnation by adding one word to that phrase. We can say to ourselves, I can't take that—yet! This acknowledges our present state, but begins to generate the momentum to transform us beyond it.

Let us return to the major and minor electromagnetic disturbances, and look at the forms they may take. Today mental institutions are crowded with people with whom we do not know what to do. Schools are crowded with students with whom teachers do not know what to do. In business, unfulfilled people are doing unfulfilling work. When we talk about these minor and major disturbances, we might be talking about physical disturbances or mental disturbances. In actuality, the disturbance of one state affects the other. For example, it is my opinion that those who have been placed in mental institutions do not have mental disease. I cannot perceive that there is such a thing as a mind which is diseased. Rather, I feel they have poorly functioning minds, because their bodies do not have the capacity to express the manifestations of their minds. If the body is not functional, the mental state cannot be expressed. The mind is a direction-giving entity. The body is regulated by the mind. It cannot do anything without the mind, but, likewise, the mind cannot do anything without the body. The body follows up on the directions of the mind. If the body does not have the proper comparative balance and activity of particles, it cannot express itself. The function of the mind is to direct the body to perform to its highest potential. So what could be wrong with the mind? Nothing.

For example, let us say I am a political leader. I need at least ten million people in order to have a functional political body, but I have only six thousand people under my direction. If that is all I have, my direction-giving is not 100 percent functional. But there is nothing wrong with me. In other words, there is nothing wrong with the mind of this political body. The mind is not lessened by the lack of physiological function, because the mind is not a system. It is a direction-giving energy which gives direction to the brain, the campaign manager, and the brain is the activator and interpreter of the mind's direction-giving energy.

To have a fully functioning body, I must use all aspects of my mind. I will discuss the different direction-giving aspects of the mind elsewhere. For now, I will say that just as the body has positive and negative polarities, which are responsible for forming and releasing substances, the mind has contracting and releasing directional energies, known respectively as intellect and intuition. The left side of the brain is predominantly for expressing linear and rational thought patterns; these are contractual energies. The right side of the brain is predominantly for regulating the body, processing unconscious information, and extending energies creatively; these are releasing energies. If I do not use these energies and integrate the two hemispheres of my brain for expressive, spontaneous, applied living, my body will have psychosomatic problems—not because my mind is diseased, but because my mind is not properly used!

On the other hand, if my mind is functioning as a whole, with intuitive and intellectual synchronization taking place, and I am 100 percent receiving, but I am depressed or I have other mental aberrations, then I have a somatopsychic disease. This means my body cannot respond to that perfectly functioning mind. Unfortunately, no medical schools give attention to somatopsychic disease. In such cases the body needs a boost so it may use the energy available to it; otherwise it will charge, and charge, and charge, but never discharge. This energy buildup will put wear on the body. The source of the block must be found so that mental energy can be expressed by the body.

Of course, many people have stagnated but have not been institutionalized—yet. I like to use the analogy of the body being a car and the mind being the driver of the car. Many of us drive with one foot on the accelerator and one foot on the brake. It is as if the car is equipped with a 454-cubic inch V-8 engine. That car could go 200 miles per hour with no trouble. It would purr at 200 miles per hour, but we allow it to go only 55. Rather than shift into overdrive, we drive in low gear, with the brake on, using energy to hold the engine's energy back. Pretty soon that car idles rough and runs rough, because it is not using all of its energy.

We may do this same thing to ourselves. If we feel we cannot behave the way we want to, we may modify ourselves to fit society's expectations.

Imagine you are an excited, enthusiastic person, with abundant functional energy. You have a 454-cubic inch engine under your hood. You have tuned it to perfection. Its peak performance is at 200 miles per hour. You have prepared your car and trained yourself to handle that power and that, in itself, adds to your excited state. You want to put the pedal to the floor and roar! But everyone else is trying to put their feet on your brake, because if they don't put their feet on your brake, they will appear slow and will feel rotten about that. So the authority, a traffic officer, comes into the picture, who might also fear appearing slow next to you. The traffic officer tells you to slow down or you will get a ticket or go to jail. But if you do not risk expression, soon that perfectly tuned car does not run so well, and you lose the ability to perform at peak efficiency. In short, the body cannot express the mind, because the mind cannot direct the body.

This is a society of phoniness. We are all very sophisticated, and we should look up the word *sophisticated*. It means "falseness." Sophistication impairs the physiological processes, much as we impair a car by driving with the brake on. We do not use the potential of the car, nor do we use the potential of the body. When we do not use the potential of the body, we impair the mental and emotional processes of the mind, because the mind could let the body go, but instead holds it back.

What if I go to the coffee room at work, and sit with a bunch of stuffy, sophisticated people who talk about stocks and bonds, and politics, in which I have absolutely no interest? I sit there with a wise face, nodding my head, but I think, What am I doing here? After work I dress up and go to a dinner party. I sit there with a suit on, stuffing myself with turkey, though on my own I would never wear a suit or eat turkey. I sit there because I don't want to stand out, and I tell myself it is just for a couple of hours. Meanwhile, the belt cuts into my stomach, and the turkey makes me feel queasy. Where do I get the crazy idea that acting sophisticated that many hours a day is not going to affect my body's state? The purpose of my life is not to modify my behavior for the sake of society. Rather, it is to become aware of my potentials and to totally express them without concern for the result. If I express myself in such a manner, I will have no need to try to dominate anyone, be violent, suffer from wasting illnesses, or use alcohol or drugs to escape my sophistication.

It is seemingly easier to adapt ourselves to the nonfunctioning than to the functioning, especially when we listen to nonfunctioning authorities who tell us how we should behave. We need to be our own authorities. We need to be responsible, which means "to be able to respond." We cannot afford to let anyone tell us what the world is, what is right for us to do, what is right for us to eat. That is our responsibility to ourselves. Mentally, physically, and nutritionally, we need to go beyond a belief system, which is based upon someone else's concept of "That's the way it is . . ." If we do not go beyond a belief system, we will get hung up on "the way it is" and not hear the next part of the statement, which is, "for me." This is why we need an ever–flowing, evolving knowing system based on our experiences and an understanding of our perceptions. We must become self-observant and take our observations as the basis for our knowing system and use the concepts and perceptions of others merely as a verifying factor, rather than as an authority. Then we can say, "Oh, you experienced it that way. Fantastic. But that doesn't fit with my experience. I am going to stick with my experience." Knowingness comes from personal experience and not from thinking about others' experiences. Because if we compare our experiences to those of others, we may begin to doubt if we really did experience anything. We might even give up our experiences for those of others which sound better, or more believable, or more accurate. But for all we know, the experiences of others may not even be their own. They may have gotten them from others. When we trade our lives for the experiences of others, our lives have no direction and lack energy. We get further behind by wondering what is right and slow down the momentum of our bodies by believing rather than knowing; by watching life rather than risking to be alive.

As long as we question, and compare, and hold onto thoughts without acting upon them, our radiance and health will be dimmed. How do I know this statement is true? Well, let's look at the activity and chemistry of the brain, and how I believe the brain treats thoughts which we hold onto.

The pineal was once thought to be nonfunctional, or a vestigal organ, but entire books are now written about the pineal, and the activity and the regulation provided by its hormones. The pineal is located between the two hemispheres of the brain. Among the hormones the pineal secretes is serotonin. Serotonin is a neurotransmitter inhibitor. In other words, it is the brake, or the guard. When you hold onto a thought, serotonin inhibits its vitality. It becomes like a caged animal. The thought has vitality, but you do not allow it to use that vitality. If serotonin is continuously used to inhibit thoughts, in time there may not be enough serotonin available to keep your reason functioning, or provide the necessary checks on other neural activities. The serotonin cages the thoughts, because you are the one who has chosen to de–liberate. And what does the word *de–liberate* mean? *Liberate* means "to free." *De-liberate* means "to take away freedom." You have chosen to take away the freedom of your thoughts and not allow them to be expressed. As you pack more of these thoughts into their cages, they get wilder, they get cramped, and soon they need more regulation. So you are forced to call in your reserves, which is your dopamine.

Dopamine is a product of the hormone epinephrine, which is produced in the medulla of the adrenal glands. Dopamine's primary function is to act as a messenger. It gives direction to nerve impulses to assure the body responds properly to stimuli. When dopamine is called upon to back up the serotonin by sedating caged thoughts, necessary body responses will not occur. For example, if your little toe gets a stimuli to wiggle, but the messenger of that action is busy taming animals, that little toe will never wiggle.

Serotonin when used to guard thoughts and dopamine when used to tame them, do not allow thoughts to express themselves freely and nourish them. Nutrients and energy, such as oxygen and glucose, are diverted from the rest of the body in order to feed these caged thoughts. This takes away from the rest of the activity of the body.

Holding onto thoughts is mental constipation. It usually is accompanied by intestinal constipation, because an excess of energy is in the brain. This creates a deficiency in the colon, so there is less activity taking place in the colon. In other words, the food in the intestines is not properly digested. It is not activated. And how did the energy get to the caged animals in the brain? By the only transportation the body has: the blood. The blood not only takes the nutrients to the brain, thereby diverting them from tissues and organs which otherwise would be manufacturing new substances, but the blood also collects the garbage created from chemical activities. The blood knows which treatment plant, meaning the liver and kidneys, gets which garbage. But when an excess of nutrients and blood go to the brain to feed the animals and collect their waste, imagine what happens to the rest of the body. In the first place, the vitality of the caged animals has become toxic to the body. Second, the body is no longer moving in an appropriate way. Food is not being digested, so the energy of the food is not being activated. As the body is loaded with good materials which are not being used, those materials become garbage too, garbage called toxins.

This brings us face to face with one reason why we should never be self-righteous. When we are self-righteous we hold onto our opinions. Our ceaseless judgment blocks our spontaneity and impairs our metabolism. Some people are malnourished because they hold onto their thoughts. They dare not be spontaneous. Spontaneity is part of our nutritional activity. Without it, the best substances can become toxic to our body.

Most people lie in bed for eight hours, holding onto nutrients, which causes a predominantly negative charge. They even wake up with a sour taste in the mouth. They do not realize they are predominantly acidic, because they have been working the whole night, but doing nothing. They immediately begin to think about work. They think about what they have done or what they have to do. They do not immerse themselves in expression that day. They do not creatively express themselves at work. They do not creatively express themselves at home. All day, every day, they hold back—mentally, physically, and emotionally.

It matters not what the activity is. It can be anything that acts out what comes in, but it should be spontaneous, without question, and without concern for the result. The act should give you joy and enable you to give joy. Activity is the key. Activity sustains you. It allows your biochemical processes to continually activate energy encapsulated in molecules, so nothing stagnates in your body. That energy has a flow that is directed outward from the body and you *radiate* energy. Your expression and your radiance are enhanced by the full involvement of your body, mind, heart, and spirit, and *that* will keep you healthy.

The molecular state, which is only one state of the entire transformation process, is generally the only state considered when we consider our physical health. But the molecular state is not the terminal product of our activities. When we allow it to become the terminal product, we can become terminally ill. The molecular state within the body takes place in order that form can be temporarily maintained so energy can be released again, and that is why the forming and transforming processes must be ongoing. As we continue to transform ourselves and move to higher and higher energy levels, we evolve through our involvement. It is the same for all the particles we take in. If we do not transform them into an energy state higher than what they were when we took them in, if we dilute them, we impede their involvement and evolvement. So I return to an idea I advanced in Chapter 1: The universe is responsible for us, as we are responsible for the universe.

A metaphor often used in churches beautifully shows the essence of expressing without concern for results. Jesus is portrayed as a man who walks over God's green acres. He carries a sack of seed. As he walks he keeps throwing out seeds, but he never looks back to see whether the seeds settle in the soil, because he knows a lot of the seeds he throws out will be eaten by birds. The same is true of us. Much of what we throw out will be eaten by birds, but instead of looking back we worry about it. Jesus was not worried because he knew the birds would eat the seeds that did not settle on fertile soil. The birds would digest them and throw their droppings upon the seeds that *had* settled on fertilized soil. He did not hesitate to continue what he was spontaneously doing, because he knew nature would do what was necessary.

The same thing is true of your mind and body. Not only do you impede the proper functioning of your mind through ignorance of how its energy works, you impede the proper functioning of your body by not living spontaneously. You have a wise body, but fears and opinions can damage it. You think, Oh no! I have not eaten this. What will this do to my body? What will it not do to my body? Opinions of what is good and what is bad, or what is right and what is wrong, stagnate the processes of transformation. There are no bad foods. There are only good foods. All foods have both positive and negative charges. When a person absorbs too much of one or the other, it destroys what is functional. Whether you should eat a particular food depends upon whether you are in an appropriate state, physically, mentally, and emotionally, to metabolize that food.

Chapter 3

Expressing

There are many systems which name and describe personality types, body types, and mind–body types. In this chapter I discuss the four humors, recommending diets based on them. I use this system because it is one of the oldest, having its roots in early Greek medicine. It was embraced by medicine until the 1900s, when medicine became the domain of specialists, who were concerned only with specific organs, structures, or diseases. Another reason I use this system is that it considers the relationship between mental states and physical states.

Not surprisingly, considering its ancestry, the system of humors embodies characteristics of the four primal elements— air, fire, water, and earth. In the body these elements are represented by the four radical states of energy: light, heat, moisture, and crystallization. How these states of energy are transformed and transported through the body has been briefly discussed in the preceding chapters. Among the ways the four elements are expressed in the body are by the actions of the four cardinal humors, or body fluids: blood, lymph, yellow bile, and black bile. The mind–body types associated with these humors are known respectively as sanguine, choleric, phlegmatic, and melancholic.

In this system of mind–body types, the degree of interaction among these humors is said to be responsible for one's health, stature, and disposition. Of course, because all four humors are present in every body, few people exhibit only those characteristics associated with any one type, but the influence of one of the humors is frequently more predominant and noticeable than the other three. Being aware of our tendencies, pitfalls, and potentials helps us become more expressive, involved, and healthful. This system can become part of a larger method to help you determine your nutritional needs.

These four mind–body types are general classifications. The humors system is a simple approach from which we can create examples of how mind–body types operate in order to better understand ourselves and others. I will not discuss what it means to have a stout neck, broad forehead, or square shoulders, or how many bumps each of us has on the head. All of these things could give some indication as to the group to which we belong, but I have little interest in the form of the body. I prefer to investigate the function of the body, because what is important is the physiological action in relation to the mental state, and the mental state in relation to the physiological action. In short, how well does a person's body implement the direction-giving energy of the mind in order to fulfill that person's function. We must take the whole individual into consideration, recognizing that the functions of the glands, hormones, nerves, blood, heart, lungs, kidney, spleen, pancreas, brain, muscles, and everything else in the body all interrelate. So we will never see an organ or a system function as it is described in a textbook. All the organs and all the physiological systems strive to interrelate, and operate in order to fulfill an individual's potentials.

For example, one person might have hyperthyroidism compared with a textbook person. But is the thyroid really overactive, or does it only seem overactive because that person needs that extra activity? We may well find out that if that person had a less active thyroid, she couldn't function appropriately! Perhaps that person is a natural-born leader, and requires that extra activity in order to lead, which is her function. If this leader's thyroid were "normal," then it would not be able to metabolize her energy, and she would not be able to perform her function. If she could not perform her function, her mind–body would surely be less radiant and she would be unfulfilled.

Table 1 lists the four humor types and their characteristics. In the table *temperament* means the mind–body condition attributed to a predominance of one of the four humors. For example, the temperament of a sanguine person is warm and moist. That means a sanguine's body is usually warm and moist to the touch. That person will also have a warm personality, and will be able to integrate well with others. A person with warm personality will allow reactions and relationships between himself and others to occur. The moist and dry aspects also refer to the intensity with which a person is involved either inwardly or outwardly. The more intensive a person is with his particular aspects, the drier will be the body as well as the personality. *Traditional* refers to the color associated with each type. *Humor* means the predominant body fluid, which influences the temperament and the physiological condition. *Organ endocrine gland* refers to the physiological structures associated with the fluid and the temperament (see Table 2). The health and temperament of a person are affected by how functional the organs associated with that fluid are. The activity of the organs affect the physical, mental, and emotional states in specific ways. Nutritional therapy and other therapies can be directed to help restore the functions of the organs if they become deficient.

Table 1
The Four Humors

Temperament	Traditional	Humor	Organ/Endrocrine Gland
Sanguine (warm and moist)	Red	Blood	Heart/Thymus
Choleric (hot and dry)	Yellow	Adrenaline	Adrenals
Phlegmatic (cold and moist)	White	Lymph	Spleen
Melancholic (cool and dry)	Black	Bile	Gallbladder/Thyroid

Table 2
Personality Traits

Sanguine	Choleric	Phlegmatic	Melancholic
easygoing	fiery	calm	sober
playful	irritable	slow	serious
talkative	vital	persistent	reserved
sympathetic	restless	considerate	anxious
sociable	aggressive	careful	depressive
hopeful	egocentric	reliable	brooding
optimistic	ardent	controlled	pessimistic
agile	idealistic	realistic	heavy
supple	supple	heavy	
changeable	changeable		

Sanguine types are active people, who need to be seen and heard. Physically, these people are typically slender, with ruddy, healthful complexions. The warm and moist classification relates to the personality as well as the physical condition.

A sanguine is usually soft, pliable, and agile. Because the blood is this type's most influential humor, everything a sanguine does comes from the heart. This personality is one of the alternating types, a type capable of changing and transmuting self, others, and energies. The heart and thymus are the fulcrum of the transmutation of energies, which is constantly occurring in the body. This transmutation allows the sanguine to be pliable and agile, traits related to being able to change and adapt. The thymus embodies the primal element of air, manifested in the body as light. The thymus regulates the immune system and thereby consciousness, for the greater your consciousness and radiance, the higher your resistance to anything of a lower energy.

Because sanguines have such an active nature, they are fast oxidizers. *Oxidizing* means "activating the processes of digestion, assimilation and metabolism." These active, activating people are very sociable. Their characteristics include being easygoing, carefree, and optimistic. Some sanguines become outgoing for the approval of others and will do anything for it. They are active but insecure. They overextend themselves, and experience performance and acceptance anxieties.

For each feeling there is a physiological state where one organ is affected more than others. If insecurities prevail, sanguines will begin to develop problems in the colon area, such as ulcerative colitis, cancer of the colon, or diverticulitis. So we can ask, What eats these people? It eats these people that they can't be perfect. Rather, it eats them that they feel they must prove themselves all the time. So the colon first becomes spastic, then atonic, then ulcerative. Or these people could get heavy in the belly, but still be slender elsewhere. Their need for approval can develop into undue and unalleviated stress which, not surprisingly, can lead to heart trouble and problems with the thymus. This need for approval is essentially a problem of consciousness. Phosphorous is important to them, because it helps get energy up from the lower endocrine glands to the thyroid, pituitary, and pineal glands. In these higher centers the energy becomes more of a stabilized expression of self, rather than a wanting to please or wanting to be involved beyond what is reasonable.

So certain diets can benefit these people. The digestive system should be clean, which will help the physiological state, but if they maintain the attitude of doing something for approval's sake, they are still being eaten by the attitude. That's like bringing your car to the garage over and over, but not changing your driving habits—then complaining that your mechanic is not very good! It is not sufficient to change the diet and make those unfunctional nutrients functional unless you also get to the cause, that is, the mental and emotional states that are not bringing out potentials. Sanguines may be either withholding them or throwing them out. So what eats these people? Their outlook on life eats them!

Choleric people are typically hot and dry. Predominantly influenced by the adrenal glands, they can function from a very emotional level. These people heat up to situations, showing more characteristics of fire than any other type. Their hot temperament fuels the potential for anger. It also fuels the potential for high involvement. They can be very vital, aggressive, and impulsive, and may become enraptured with sports or others types of competition. They can be tenacious in their pursuits and live only for them, becoming more and more passionate rather than compassionate. The martial arts can be important for them, providing both a release and a needed source of inward focus. Physically, they are fast oxidizers, which allows the body to activate the energy necessary for all their activity. This, coupled with their desire for involvement, makes them impulsive, aggressive, fiery, and idealistic.

Because of their characteristic needs for outward expression and acceptance, both the sanguine and choleric are more susceptible to hypertension than either the phlegmatic or melancholic. Susceptibility to hypertension and related disorders makes mental calmness essential. Choleric people, especially, may need to peri-odically engage in solitary activities, such as a walk on the beach or camping alone, in order to balance introspection with outward expression. Fortunately for both of these mind–body types, once they are convinced of the need for and benefits of introspection, they have the self-confidence and willpower to direct themselves in order to achieve the benefits available from yoga or other forms of relaxation and self-regulation exercises.

Phlegmatic people are predominantly influenced by the spleen. They are characterized by the element of water, which is represented by splenic secretions that modify the blood and lymph. Because of slower oxidation processes, they are more introverted than either sanguines or cholerics, and so tend to be somewhat heavy in body, mind, and spirit. The body and tem-perament generally include being cold and moist.

Phlegmatics tend to be bitter, viewing their lack of involve-ment as caused by not being accepted by others. Therefore they in turn will not be accepting of others, and will express them-selves in negative ways. They feel envy, spite, and vengeance when they hold their energies in the spleen, and don't allow them to be transformed by the higher organs. This overworks the spleen and can cause these people to become anemic, and therefore cooler, and puts an extra burden on the bone marrow to produce enough red blood cells. Arthritis may also be one of their symp-toms. On a more positive note, when these people are involved, they love their work and other people. They are persistent and reliable. They have a calming influence on the more heated types, thereby helping those types to be more directed and stable.

Melancholics are predominantly influenced by the black humor, that is, the secretions of the bile duct and gallbladder. The melancholic, as an earth sign, is sour. Melancholics are like sour grapes. They are sober, serious, and reserved, yet anxious. Although others might call them stable, I call them depressed. Because of their low state of oxidation, temperature, and expres-sion, they can be the most introverted type of all. Melancholics have a hard time generating enough mental and bodily activity to be outwardly involved. They tend to have the driest personalities and heaviest bodies. Their lack of activity makes them prone to metabolic problems associated with a hypothyroid condition. They may also be hypoglycemic.

Though melancholics may feel the need for outward expression, they are so pessimistic of their chances for success and so worried about the outcome of their activities they will hardly do anything, and will resist any type of change or optimism. You can show them a reason for optimism, but they will see a reason for pessimism even in the optimism. A sanguine will revel in the morning sunshine, while a melancholic will lament that sooner or later it is going to rain.

Melancholics, and, to a lesser degree, phlegmatics, hardly dramatize anything. If they express anything it has to be drawn out of them like taffy. They may harbor aggressiveness in the body, but have trouble expressing it appropriately. Aggressiveness gives them a tremendous capacity for action, but it is difficult for them to transform that aggressiveness. They need to learn how to heat themselves up with it, then bring that energy up to the thyroid so they express it creatively out of the body and put it as form into the world.

Though I have discussed body types associated with each classification, a person cannot be categorized simply because of how he looks. I have seen melancholic, pessimistic people who are emaciated, rather than heavy. These, especially, personify the saying, "It's not what you eat, but what eats you." They are people who need to pay more attention to what eats them, what they are worried about, why they are pessimistic, and why they cannot activate their joyful state. Food can help them, but it is not the predominant factor. To go beyond a depressed state, they need to learn how to express themselves and how to dramatize. Drama allows one to depersonalize anxieties, to put the anxieties outside of oneself, allowing oneself to act upon them, rather than being acted upon by them. Then creative transformation can ensue. The very act of such expression elevates what is being held back into a higher energy state, thereby imparting greater health to the entire organism. It is beneficial for melancholics to get involved with groups in no-lose sports, such as biking, boating, skiing, or events mentioned in the book *New Games*. Becoming active in setting up these events would also be good for them, as would theater work and art.

The self-confidence and risk-taking of sanguine and choleric people makes autogenics and biofeedback highly successful for them. It is hard, however, to bring about change through the use of autogenics or biofeedback for melancholics. Melancholics first need to get out of their depression and stagnation, or else they will say, "It will not work for me. It might work for others, but not for me." They will not do anything in competitive sports, because they will tell themselves they never win. Therapy and psychological role playing can help them accept themselves. Phlegmatic people may benefit from these activities to a lesser degree. Both melancholics and phlegmatics also need to understand the romantic aspects of relationships, which will help sweeten their respective sourness and bitterness. Having a relationship is a sign of involvement and evolvement, as is losing someone. They must understand that lost or broken relationships, painful though they are, can be the impetus for greater love, involvement, understanding, and self-knowledge. All of these activities and experiences are vital in guiding people to tune into their potentials, which in itself raises the excitement level. Then the task is to raise that excitement level to the point of expression. Of course, this expression would help stimulate and balance the thyroid, which is usually hypoactive, and generally assist metabolism, digestion, and assimilation.

Table 3 lists the nutrients each mind type needs to nourish the organs associated with the predominant humor. Table 4 discusses sources of these nutrients. The many different foods listed should aid in developing an appealing, creative diet.

Table 3
Nutritional Requirements of the Four Humors

Sanguines are susceptible to imbalances of the thymus. Nutrients required for the *thymus* are calcium, iron, fluorine, gold, and phosphorus.

Cholerics are susceptible to imbalances of the adrenals. Necessary nutrients for the *adrenal cortex* are calcium, fluorine, iron, and silicon. For the *adrenal medulla*, phosphorus, sulfur, iodine, and manganese are important.

Phlegmatics are susceptible to imbalances of the spleen and lymph system. The *spleen* needs chlorine, magnesium, potassium, and sodium. The *lymph*, as a fluid, is maintained through proper nourishment of the spleen and thymus.

Melancholics are susceptible to imbalances of the bile duct, gallbladder, liver, and thyroid. The nutrient required for the *bile duct and gallbladder* is olive oil.* For the *liver*, sodium, chlorine, potassium, magnesium, and copper are essential. Iodine, chlorine, sodium, potassium, and magnesium are crucial for the *thyroid.*

*Note: Olive oil, as a whole substance, nourishes the gallbladder. Bile methods include formulas for flushing and nourishing the liver, spleen, and gallbladder, and contain olive oil. It is interesting to note that there are hardly any gallstone operations or gallbladder removals, or gallbladder diseases in Greece or Italy, even for melancholic people, where olive oil is used extensively in cooking.

Table 4
Food Sources of Nutrients

Calcium: milk; milk products; green, leafy vegetables; shellfish; molasses; bone meal.

Chlorine: table salt; seafood; meats; ripe olives; rye flour; dulse.

Copper: organ meats; seafood; shellfish; nuts; legumes; molasses; raisins; bone meal.

Fluorine: tea; seafood; bone meal.

Gold: shellfish; seafood; red beets; root vegetables.

Iodine: dulse; kelp; Irish moss; seafood; shellfish.

Magnesium: seafood; whole grains; dark green vegetables; molasses; nuts; bone meal.

Manganese: whole grains; green, leafy vegetables; legumes; nuts; pineapple; egg yolks.

Sodium: table salt; seafood; baking powder; baking soda; celery; milk products; seaweeds in general, for example, kelp and dulse.**

Sulfur: fish; eggs; onions; garlic; meats; cabbage; brussels sprouts.

**Phlegmatics may take kelp or any other seaweed to get iodine to stabilize the thyroid. Melancholics should not take kelp to obtain iodine, as kelp has a calming effect on hyperthyroidism, a condition not found in melancholics.*

Influences Upon the Mind–Body Type

There are many influences which collectively determine the mind–body type. At birth a person is already in a predominant state. We are becoming more aware of how influential the outer environment is upon a developing fetus, especially the environment of the parents and the consciousness of the parents. First, let's look at what the word *environment* means. *Environ* means "to encircle." *Ment* means "the mind or mental state." So *environment* means "that which encircles the mind." The environment and the individual function for which a person is being born influences the mental state of the fetus. This individual function includes specific tools and potentials which can be suppressed or enhanced by parental words, attitudes, and actions. If the parents say their baby will become a banker, or a lawyer, or a mechanic, when the child came to this world to be an artist or a warrior, the child may have to work through extra guilt, anxiety, or anger in order to actualize herself.

By hypnotizing adults and guiding them back to the prenatal state, researchers have discovered that frequently the fetus is aware of and recognizes virtually everything which occurs to the mother and itself during gestation. The mental states of the mother, father, and other people who form significant relationships with the fetus influence its predominant mind–body type. The mind–body type of a person may change, depending upon how the person matures and the types of relationships that person develops. Maturing can be equated with how a person meets challenges. Maturity develops simultaneously with relationships with self, relationships with others, and relationships with the environment. The mind–body is also influenced by the type and extent of support a person receives while discovering the potentials he has to deal with challenge and create change. Expressing one's potentials is probably the single most powerful way to maintain health.

Unfortunately, we kill many of the talents that children possess. Parents can be so proud when their children show an interest in something that they begin to stuff it down their children's throats, forcing them to train, train, train, and to do the task the way an outside authority tells them. Conversely, parents may show no interest or discourage their children when a child's activity or behavior could be giving both child and parent an idea of the child's function. In either case the parent may overshadow the child's inner needs and inner authority, thereby affecting the mind–body type predominant in the child. This will affect the child's nutritional needs. Of course, how the child challenges and responds to family influences will also affect the environment, as well as her development.

For example, when I was challenged I took the challenge. When I was told not to do certain things, I questioned why I was not supposed to do them, and I experimented. I did whatever I was told not to do to discover how truthful those authorities were. I found that for every one hundred things they told me I couldn't do, I could do ninety-nine of them without adverse consequences. I pushed continuously to bring out my potentials.

So, although we are not locked into a specific way of behaving or a destiny, we do have inherent potentials which indicate our function. To an extent these potentials are revealed by the incoming energy known as the ray. In *Human Energy Systems* I detailed some of the qualities associated with the seven principal rays, the colors which coincide with the main colors of the spectrum, and the combinations in which rays appear.

Through many years of observing people's energy fields and their rays, I have been able to equate the rays with certain human qualities and potentials. I refer to the ray as a person's toolbox. The hue, composition, and form of each ray is as unique as each person is, which means there are countless ways that potentials associated with each ray can be expressed. The ray, which enters the human energy field from above the head, penetrates the body at the crown of the skull. By placing your palm on your crown, you can feel an area which is warmer than the rest of your head. This warm spot is where your ray enters your body. The more you express its potentials, the better nourished you will be.

The ray, then, indicates a person's potentials and predominant function. There is also some relationship between the rays and the four mind–body types. For example, people operating on the green ray will not throw temper tantrums when they get upset. Green ray people, who are cool anyway, go off by themselves to cool off even more. Or they will open their mental refrigerator and throw "icicle eyes" at everyone. A person on the purple ray will become aggressive, and tell whoever is bothering her to shut up. A pink ray person will throw a tantrum, and then get more upset if people do not respond to that, because that is the way pink ray people get others' attention. So the rays give hints as to people's functions, behavior, and how their bodies operate. I don't think you can find a sanguine or choleric person on the green ray. Green ray people are phlegmatic or melancholic. A purple ray person, who can be forceful, domineering, and activating, could be sanguine or choleric. It depends how the body operates, such as if the blood really gets boiling or just gets warm. Pink ray people may be either choleric or melancholic, because even though they can be full of love and devotion or be impulsive or energetic, which are choleric traits, they can also be sacrificers and martyrs, which are melancholic traits.

For each function of life, we need a specific state of energy. So we need a specific state of health for the body's organs, which have to activate, stabilize, or, in some cases, decelerate the processes of the physical and mental transformation, which are responsible for a person being able to express himself appropriately. Classifying people by ray, or body type, or any other system is a very general approach. Never lose sight of the uniqueness of each person. Any classification should be used only as an aid to help us focus on ourselves to determine our needs or to help us suggest to someone else how she may learn to help herself. Therefore, mass diets will not work, because mass systems of classifying do not work. To help ourselves we have to know that the specifics of any state of mind affect a specific organ's state, which then affects every process of metabolism. Every state of mind and every emotion can lead to either a flow or a stagnation of energy.

Love, for example, can be so conditional before it is released that it is as much of a stagnation as jealousy, envy, or resentment.

Genetics also affects mind–body type. I think, however, that we often place more emphasis on genetics than is warranted, and too little emphasis on the immune system. Genetics combined with environment has definitely influenced racial and ethnic traits and behaviors, as well as the more specific traits and behaviors of families. And because genes allow us to adapt to a particular environment, over time a population's genes can change, thereby not limiting a population to the genetic structure of the past.

Unfortunately, though, we are allowing genetics to become a stronger source of self-limitation than ever before. I like to look at our genetic structure as a fantastic type of start-up system and back-up system. Essentially, genes are a chemical history of the physical self and of our physical ancestry. They provide for the growth and regulation of our bodies and set initial parameters for our behavior. But genetic structure is only one way through which we respond to the environment, and is only one source of our potentials. We must abide by our genetic structure *only until we transcend it.*

Often people say things such as "My father was bald so I will be bald." Or, "My mother was an alcoholic, so I am apt to be an alcoholic." These conditions are not genetic, but these people behave as if they are by identifying with the condition and feeling as though they must express them. Some doctors believe cancer is latent within all of us, waiting for the conditions under which it can be expressed. I agree with them to a large extent. The body cannot be infected or affected by something unless it has the potential to be, which we could say is genetic. We have both the potential to be diseased and the potential to be healthy, because we have the choice to express ourselves or to allow ourselves to stagnate. If we choose to identify with the thought that a disease is genetic, and hold onto that thought, then the mind and body become dominated by that thought. And in time the body may express that dominance as disease.

Suppose I assume a particular disease, say alcoholism, to be purely genetic, because my father and his father were both afflicted with it. So to stay healthy I just have to be extra careful not to do this or that, or I will fall victim to alcoholism too. With that attitude I am essentially saying, I cannot transcend my genetic structure. But that is a ridiculous statement. If we could not transcend our genetic structure, we would still be Neanderthals, doing as they did.

We are not Neanderthals because we have transcended that genetic structure. We have evolved. But remember, we cannot evolve unless we get involved. By living as though genetic doom lurked within, by living fearfully, I am not involving myself to my fullest potential. I am not trying to discover if that doom is valid for me. So I stay completely away from alcohol, thus never being able to prove to myself that although I drink I am not an alcoholic. I will never know. So I impair myself mentally, and ascribe little value to my immune system and my ability to transcend this "genetic" thing.

Allow me to use myself as an example again. I should have tuberculosis because, as a boy, I did the opposite of everything my parents told me to do in order to avoid it. They told me to wear a cap to keep my head warm, or else I would get tuberculosis. So I wore one until I got far enough from the house that they could not see me, and then I took it off. They told me to wear socks long enough to cover my legs and knees, but I rolled them down. They told me to keep my feet dry. My feet were always wet from jumping canals, something all Dutch boys do. They got wet in the morning and stayed wet all day in school. When I went home my feet got wet again jumping back over the canals. But I kept a pair of dry shoes and socks in the toolshed, which I put on before I went into my house. I did all those things to prove to myself that if I did not get tuberculosis it was not because I wore a cap, or kept my socks up, or kept my feet dry. I got involved with experiments to prove to myself I would not get tuberculosis if I did not follow another's authority or belief.

Of course, there are differences between the influence of genetic structure on a person and his family and the influence of genetic structure on an ethnic population. For example, many Asians and blacks are not able to digest cow's milk because, in their history, they normally would have drunk only mother's milk. Therefore, cow's milk is toxic to them because their bodies lack the enzyme lactase, which breaks down milk sugar. But that is the wisdom of the body. It gives nothing in excess, but expresses what is needed in order to survive in a particular environment. As more blacks and Asians make dairy products part of their diets, we have begun to see a reduction of the toxic effects of milk upon their bodies. These groups are gradually transcending genetic structure, a process which usually takes longer when a group is affected than when a trait is expressed by an individual or family.

Just as entire populations can be susceptible to certain traits, entire populations can be immune to certain diseases. For example, Indonesians swim in, cook with, and drink the same untreated water which carries their wastes and the wastes of their livestock, but they are unaffected by it. Their immune systems can handle that, but most Europeans and Americans would get sick from that water. In certain groups of Eskimos and Japanese fishers, arthritis is unknown because they ingest fish liver oil every day. The oil keeps the bones and joints lubricated, and it nourishes the liver, making the body less susceptible to the toxins which lead to arthritis. But if some of us were transported to the wet and the cold, we might become arthritic no matter how much fish oil we consumed, because an inflexible mental perception of cold would continue to tell us our joints should be swollen and stiff. Others would learn to thrive in the cold. These people would eventually create a new genetic expression based upon changed physical, mental, and emotional states.

The world is changing much faster now than ever. We will require a new genetic system in order to be able to fully operate in this changing environment. That will be possible only by transcending our present state. We must develop our existing potentials to adapt to pollutants in water, air, soil, and food. Though I prefer the natural world and prefer to consume natural substances instead of synthetics, I also prefer to be healthy. At this stage of our consciousness, I can be healthy only by being unaffected by the toxins in the environment. One day we may not have enough oxygen available in the atmosphere for life processes to continue in the way they do today. We may have to adapt to having less oxygen, the same as we do when we are high in the mountains. We may even have to learn to live on new substances in the atmosphere in order to support our metabolisms. We can train ourselves to live on less oxygen, as we can train ourselves to live on less food, getting some of our nutrients through resonating with more subtle forms of these nutrients. We need to understand the processes in which we are already involved. In that way we will gain a better understanding of how to nourish and express ourselves and how to evolve.

The social environment exerts an influence upon us comparable to that of genetics. Both have a tremendous impact if we put emphasis on them. At this moment the social environment is dominated by fear: fear of poor economic conditions, fear of war, fear of cancer, fear of AIDS. Couples who have been married and faithful to one another for twenty years are beginning to restrain their sexual intimacy because of fear of AIDS, not realizing the common cold results from an acquired immune deficiency too. If people continue to be victimized by fear, it will have a detrimental effect upon the health of the general population. But this need not happen. We can be in control of our lives and in control of our environment. At this time the environment controls us. That is why the world immune system is deficient.

Why should we not be affected by the diseases and conditions of our rapidly changing environment? Because any disease which can harm the body occurs at an amplitude which is weaker than that of a healthy body. When you hold onto fear, you slow down the processes of energy transformation, causing you to become sympathetic to and resonate with these lower energies. As the body becomes less radiant, less resistant to disease, you attract more stagnations and maladies. That reinforces your fear that if you do such and such or get near such and such, then you will get ill too, because the disease is contagious. That's right! It is contagious, but it is also contagious to attach yourself to a higher, fearless state of energy, one which trusts the body to sustain the processes of transformation without incident.

We can view genetics and the environment as parts of the hierarchy of energy systems in which we simultaneously operate. As with any energy system, they can affect us or we can affect them. We can use our genes and the environment to express the more refined and subtle aspects of our beingness, of which they provide the raw materials, or, by imposing limits on ourselves, we can stagnate expression and cause eventual disease.

The state of consciousness is related to the state of health, because consciousness is directly responsible for what we express. A higher state of health means that the body is operating at a rate closer to its optimal level. So when a healthy body is infected by something, its immune systems will immediately recognize it and quickly perform all the physiological steps necessary to dissolve that infection. Your immune system has the capacity to destroy anything which is foreign to your body.

Succeeding chapters of this book will describe ways by which you can know your inner and outer environments, and increase your understanding of the processes of and organs for energy transformations occurring within you, thereby attaining greater health and greater control over what eats you.

Most medical studies add to already existing fears. When we read the list of foods and food additives which cause cancer, it seems there is no longer anything safe to eat. This is not surprising when we realize that anything which the body cannot break down or cannot use becomes toxic to it. Cancer is one way the body responds to toxins which it cannot break down. If the body is not radiant, such things as apples, brown rice, spinach, turkey, or any other seemingly "good foods" which are not metabolized can cause cancer.

Look at statistics on subjects of medical research, or look at statistics on victims of environmental disasters. We find, for example, that ten years ago 10 percent of a group of people living around a toxic waste dump gave birth to children with birth defects. Today 20 percent of this group has had abnormal births. Yes, these figures are alarming, but never are those who have been unaffected studied. Never do we measure the voltage emanating from the affected and unaffected people. If we did, we would find, without exception, that no affected person had a higher electrical output than an unaffected person. The unaffected person has a much greater control of and harmony with the environment and with the self. The unaffected person is much more involved, joyful, and expressive as well.

I have been a white rat in laboratories throughout the world in order to prove these principles to myself. I have been connected to virtually every type of biofeedback and biometric instrument there is, demonstrating how the body can maintain its health through radiance. I have been injected with cancerous tissues and toxic substances. I have been impaled with rusty nails and unsterilized knitting needles. Not once have I suffered an infection. All of us have the ability to awaken these potentials within us. We need not be restrained by limiting thought represented by genetics, the environment, or other people. When we allow our potentials to flow, we begin to affect our environment and everything which would otherwise be affecting us. You could say we infect the environment with our radiance, energizing the environment and raising the resistance level of whomever we meet.

All of us need unconditional love. Everything is based upon that. I like to use the word LOVE as an acronym. The *L* is for life and the *O* is for omnipresent, so life is present in all. In the Scriptures its says that energy is omnipresent. Yes, we say, that sounds good, but it is not present in this or that.

People have walked out of my lectures when I have said the table at which they were sitting was made of the same energy as they. "What an insult!" they huffed. It was as if I were calling them tables. I was not calling the table a human being. I was not calling the human being a table. I said it was made up of the same energy, only it had a different formula, and therefore a different function. They and the table were interrelating, just as they were interrelating with everyone else and everything else in that room because of the omnipresent energy there.

When we talk about love and unconditional love, we start to include and exclude people and things. The slightest thing a person does against us causes us to exclude her from our category of unconditional love. Judgment is what really holds us back from unconditional love.

The V stands for victoriously, which means if I cannot be offended, then I do not need a defense. It is interesting that when I defend myself, I am actually causing the immune system to stagnate. I have pulled everything in to defend myself, thereby placing myself in the power of fear, guilt, and anxieties. Sure, there is a lot of change taking place in our world. Sure, we do not agree with all of the changes. Sure, there are situations each of us would change, because we have different opinions and functions. But do we have to be affected by all these things? Isn't it time for us to become knowing, radiant people and instead affect the world? This implies confronting risks, ridicule, and fear. This is where the E in LOVE comes in. It stands for experience. Fear becomes an incentive; it arouses the courage needed to experience life. Instead of saying, "Oh, my God, I'm afraid of taking that risk," you can say, "Fantastic! At least I now know what I'm afraid of." Then ask yourself how to face it, challenge it, act upon it. And you will see that your fear was a marvelous warning signal to let you know to get on the ball.

Look at the people who are absolutely down, depressed, repressed, suppressed, oppressed, and are affected by it. Watch them get prematurely old before your eyes. Then witness a person who challenges life and has no time to think about the odds, but simply goes out and challenges those odds. That person gets younger and younger. All of us have the chance to keep our energy flowing, but that cannot be done unless we give up our judgments and cease comparing one person with another. We judge and compare continuously.

If you want your immune system and everything which is interrelated with it to never be deficient, then look at what is causing the anxiety, stress, anger, guilt, or lack of involvement that affects and infects you, leading to stagnation. Life is an adventure! We do it an injustice when we try to tame it and eliminate everything which challenges us or causes us to feel stress. Stress too is a necessity. It is a part of the law of life. It prods you to keep alert. And remember, you can't shoot an arrow from a slack bow.

Between each of the 750 trillion cells in your body, there is a little bit of space. That space keeps the cells in a state of stress, which keeps their motion and communication going. Have you ever seen a group of people who are together because a computer said they would be compatible? Have you ever seen any growth from their relationships? It's rare, because those people are so similar. There is no stress, no spark. Have you ever had a fire or light without a spark first? We need stress, but when it becomes excessive and we do not adapt ourselves but only try to avoid it, we avoid fire. We avoid light. The ill health which follows is too high a price to pay for a seemingly secure, risk-free life. Stress can be a stimulant when we face it, not with knowledge, but with knowingness and openness. Knowingness cannot come from hearing about life from somebody else or from thinking about it. Your potentials and your environment provide ceaseless opportunities for knowingness. Knowingness comes only from experience. Through experience comes the power to make change and take charge as bit by bit you activate your potentials.

Choosing what you eat is more than a physical choice. As you gain a more intimate understanding of the processes of life and of health, and as your potentials are activated through experience, your food needs will change. But if you are not sensitive to the fact that as you enter different life stages and stages of expression your food needs change, you may merely see a need to go on a diet, because your body does not look as fashionable or as fit as society says it should. One problem with dieting is that if you feel forced to do it, the diet will rule your mental and emotional states. That will affect your ability to properly metabolize your food. Cooking and eating should bring you joy, because cooking and eating are parts of the transformation and creative processes.

Determining what you should eat is more than a physical choice. Choosing what to eat requires emotional involvement. If you become bored or irritated with your diet, those are signs telling you that something is not right for you at that particular time. The greatest thing you can do for your body at such moments is avoid eating what upsets you, no matter how good it is for you. How can it be good for you when it causes you to feel aversion? You can be sure that for every food which is "good for you," there are several other healthy foods which will excite you, and thus be much better for you. No diet makes sense if it does not give you enjoyment and the feeling that it is beneficial for you, physically, mentally, and emotionally.

Many people who have the good sense to avoid doing something or consuming something about which they are not in agreement then feel guilt. They feel they have no self-discipline. To me, being disciplined means I am a disciple of that which my inner nature says through my mind and body. But the word *discipline* registers in most people's subconscious mind as punishment, as someone else having authority over you rather than you exercising your inner knowingness. So for those of you who wish to have a healthy diet, but listen to every authority but yourselves in trying to attain it, ask yourselves, How well does this work for me? The diet does not work for you if your intentions are different from your capacity to embody it and follow it, if you find that after a couple of days that "good food" is stuck in your throat. If you feel you are being punished by that diet, or you feel you must punish yourself, so you go on a diet, then immediately the benefit of the diet is gone. No food can do anything for you if you are not in agreement with it.

Listening to yourself and diagnosing yourself are the two best ways of determining a healthy diet. A healthy diet changes as you change, and helps you activate the energies which you need activated. Most important, an individualized diet is one of the first and best steps in helping you develop the ability to know yourself and express yourself in the most dynamic ways possible. Be patient enough to permit yourself to change.

Our confusion about what is good for us, what we want, and what we need is largely related to poor diet. Improper diet also makes us more susceptible to negative factors in the environment. Many studies document the relationship of behavior to diet. Poor nutrition, specifically refined carbohydrates, is a prime cause of crime, especially sexual crimes. Children's inability to learn, teachers' inability to educate, workers' inability to produce, and our propensity, as a nation, to flip-flop from fad to fad, have a lot to do with the empty calories we ingest as refined carbohydrates, especially refined sugar. We must use active calories, derived from the few healthy foods we eat, to metabolize the empty calories; so we operate under a net energy loss, because so much of the food we eat requires more energy to be broken down and eliminated than it supplies. This puts a tremendous burden on the liver, pancreas, kidneys, and gallbladder, which transform and eliminate the toxins. With an excessive amount of activity and energy centered in the abdominal area, there is simply not enough nourishment available for the rest of the body. Metabolism becomes spasmodic and the brain has less ability to implement the directional energy of the mind.

If metabolism is thrown off, the thyroid malfunctions. Interestingly, the thyroid is the center of volitional energy, or willpower. If the thyroid is malfunctioning, the ability for stable self-expression is adversely affected, making us more susceptible to whatever else is in the environment. Does the thyroid start to malfunction because a person did not trust inner authority and did not express herself, or does it malfunction because she did not eat the proper foods, which would have allowed the thyroid to function properly? The situations cannot really be separated. It's a question of, Which comes first: the chicken or the egg?

As a prisoner of war in World War II, I witnessed Nazi atrocities firsthand. This extreme sadism could not have happened had Hitler's generals and advisers not been fed enormous quantities of pastries and other foods loaded with refined carbohydrates. Hitler himself was very selective about what he ate. He ate mostly fresh fruits and vegetables and seldom drank anything other than herbal teas. Yet when he called his deputies together, he would never speak with them until they had gorged themselves on pastries. He knew sugars and white flour starved the brain and made his people more susceptible to his will. By reducing the will, it becomes possible to essentially blot out a person's identity, making it possible for that person to commit acts he previously would have considered reprehensible.

Much research has been done on the connection between diet and personality; one excellent book on the subject is *Sugar Blues*, a book published by E. P. Dutton. Political groups are aware of the relationship between food and behavior. This is why I feel a bit of a chill run down my spine when I see pastries lined up for people to eat before they hear a speaker at a seminar, conference, or business meeting or see jelly beans being passed around by a person before a meeting.

Chapter 4

Life, Health, and the Pursuit of Happiness

The brain wave states, or extended states of consciousness, in which a person operates have a great impact on health and expression.

From birth to adolescence to adulthood, the brain wave state in which we function has a tendency to go from a predominantly delta/theta state, one in which there is mind–body harmony, to a predominantly beta state in which energy is spent questioning rather than expressing; in other words, holding back our potentials. Being in a low-amplitude beta state is considered normal for adults. Normal, yes, but it certainly is not natural! Being predominantly in low-amplitude beta is one of the greatest detriments to health.

There are three sources for what we express. We can express what society feels is appropriate for us, in which case we may as well not be here at all. Or we can be mere egotists, whereby what we express is determined by what we can gain from it. Or finally, we can express our unique potentials and connection with the universe according to what each of us as individuals perceives. That is to say, we can express what has been called the Thou Self, the higher self, the transpersonal self, or the universal self, flavoring that expression with our uniqueness, communicating with the transpersonal self while creating our own realities. Which of these sources we choose to express, and the power of that expression, determines, to a large extent, our health and radiance, as well as our experiences. We cannot separate our health from our consciousness. Both are partly determined by the source of our perceptions and our expressions thereof.

The predominant brain wave state in which most people operate usually changes according to how old they are. But it is not so much age as the state of consciousness which causes the change. Science and medicine assume that we are supposed to go from being in a predominantly delta/theta state as infants to a predominantly beta state as adults. But this change is learned, and it occurs at the expense of health and happiness. Someone who is in a predominantly beta state is holding a lot back.

In terms of cycles per second, the frequency of a particular type of brain wave tends to correspond with the age at which the brain wave appears. Infants one to two years old are in a predominantly delta/theta state, a state which occurs when mind and body are in harmony. The delta state occurs at one to four cycles per second. Little harm can come to young bodies, because the brain and mind do not question anything yet. Harm comes to the body mostly because of the thought we give it. As adults we are supposed to be in mind–body harmony only when we are in deep sleep, so we are never supposed to be conscious when we are in harmony!

The theta state generally occurs at four to seven cycles per second, and predominates in children from birth until about the age of seven. This is the time when children have the greatest capacity to express themselves uniquely, because they do not have sufficient reasoning ability to question themselves. It is a state of consciousness in which the child is concerned with refining the body he began creating in the womb to make it more capable of expressing his function in life. As theta is also a nonjudgmental state, it does no editing of what is observed and experienced. The brain records everything the child perceives and the child perceives everything happening in his environment, especially how people work with life.

By the age of seven, the alpha state begins to predominate. It is a time when children become more indoctrinated into societal and familial expectations. Alpha operates anywhere from seven to thirteen cycles per second.

During this time the body is not merely concerned with growth, but with growth and maintenance. Consequently, alpha is the body-regulating state, the state through which the subconscious mind regulates physiological processes such as heart rate and breathing. It is also the state through which the subconscious mind interprets information and experiences which occurred before birth and during infancy, including phobias, complexes, and positive affirmations which began then. I call this subconscious information the archives. It influences how information from other sources, such as from the transpersonal self, are interpreted and expressed. As theta becomes less predominant, the body changes into a form less capable of expressing functions of the higher self. The child is predominantly in alpha until the age of thirteen, an age when expectations, social and peer pressures, and responsibilities begin to dominate.

Thirteen is the age at which the beta state begins to be predominant, a state associated with reason and analytical thought. We need to be able to reason in order to express ourselves appropriately and to give our intuition direction and form. But those who are dominated by beta have a mental state that is ordinarily one of constant, low-power chatter. It is a state of questioning, rather than acting, and of not being tuned into intuition. Intuition may be received, but not recognized. Involvement with life is reduced and the richness of experience lessened. Expression is more conditional.

The ideal situation is to have all the brain wave states operating simultaneously, with each gaining in amplitude, as we become excited by seeing our potentials expressed in the world. The less we question and judge ourselves and others, the greater will be our radiance.

Too often we struggle to give form to the expectations of society, which we begin to take on as our expectations of ourselves, rather than giving life to our own ideas. This struggle affects the form of our bodies. We assume society's texture rather than expressing ourselves. The degree of our activity and the degree to which we subjugate ourselves for the sake of the approval of others determines our state of health. We embody this struggle as dis-ease. How the body expresses its dis-ease is determined by where specific stagnations occur.

Now let's see how each individual state of beingness affects her life stages and experiences, beginning with the prenatal state.

Proper fetal development is dependent not only upon the physiological health of the mother, but the mental and emotional environments created by the mother and father and, to a lesser extent, close family members. Most information written on this subject is general guidelines. Why? Because the determination of individual needs is simply too complex a subject. To a certain extent general guidelines can also be equated with belief systems, which are systems of behavior for the general population, but have no great bearing on individual needs and changes. In this chapter, therefore, I shall talk about the processes involved with the ongoing creation and expression of individual potentials from the standpoints of life stages, health, and happiness.

During pregnancy the mother's physical, emotional, and mental states are of utmost importance to the developing fetus. These, along with her experiences, determine if the nutrients necessary for her health and her baby's health will be functional for her, and thereby available for her child to develop its body.

Metaphorically, the mother is a nutritional warehouse. Any deficiencies she has during pregnancy can well be with her child during the remainder of its life. It is like building a new wall from an old wall. If the old wall was not armored, then the new wall will not be armored unless you add armor to it. The baby could get the nutrients in which it is deficient after birth, if the need is seen, but the best possible situation is for the baby to get adequate nutrients while still in the womb.

Of course, it is desirable that all necessary nutrients be functional in the body throughout life, but the responsibility of cocreating a healthy baby makes physical, mental, emotional, and nutritional assessments even more vital for the expectant mother. Ideally, the father would also have a total health assessment, thereby acknowledging his importance in creating an environment which will foster a healthy child.

Women who start to flourish during pregnancy because of their joyful state of expectation enable their baby to have an easier time developing; the baby's nutritional and emotional environments are healthy. Certain nutritional deficiencies, however, can affect her joyful state. An expectant mother may be depressed because of a deficiency of functional potassium, a situation discussed in Chapter 2. Consequently, the baby's nervous system, which has a tremendous need for potassium in its developmental state, will be depressed too.

A nutritionist can advise the expectant mother on what foods to eat in order to provide the building blocks for her maintenance and the baby's development, but the mother needs to be content with her mental and emotional states, which have a pronounced effect on her metabolism, digestion, absorption, and assimilation. Otherwise, the raw materials will be there, the bricks, so to speak, but not the mortar, so that an adequate house can be built. Unfortunately, there are few places where the mother and father can get total health counseling and where they will be treated as individuals charged with fulfilling their unique potentials and functions. I hope this book can be one resource to help people understand the processes of transformation and health and learn how to activate potentials. Many functional nutritional deficiencies can be alleviated with tissue salts, provided the mental and emotional states also change to accompany, activate, and maintain the changing physical state.

Food cravings any time, but especially during pregnancy, are one way the body calls for help. Cravings are the body's way of saying, Hey, pay attention to me. You are telling me to do things, but not giving me what I need to do them. Cravings can be pretty strange sometimes, such as an urge for ice cream with pickles, but that is just the translation given to the body's call for help— and not a very good translation at that. We need to learn to speak the language of the body. A craving for pickles may mean a need for something acid in order to activate the body's total energy in a specific way, such as improving metabolism in the gastrointestinal area. A craving for something sweet, which may be interpreted as a desire for ice cream, means the blood sugar is low, which means kinetic energy is low. People with copper or zinc deficiencies often crave chocolate, because functional insulin or glycogen levels are low. Women who lack estrogen frequently crave licorice, which, again, is the intellectual interpretation of what the body is trying to say. Or one day a woman may need protein. She eats some red meat and it makes her nauseated. Why? Because the body could not assimilate that type of protein, so she needs to get it in a different form, such as tuna fish or egg. The next day the woman recognizes she still needs protein. This time she is able to digest the red meat, because the body is now sufficiently stimulated and balanced so it can use that protein source. Food cravings indicate that something is eating you, and that you need to become a productive consumer, rather than a consumed producer.

There are also cravings to eat for the sake of eating or to sleep for the sake of sleeping. These activities tend to divert attention away from what is really disturbing a person. They are psychosomatic cravings, as opposed to the somatopsychic cravings just mentioned. Either type of craving can occur during pregnancy.

Depression and fatigue are already contracted states, so don't eat or sleep! Go for a brisk walk first, or else you will exacerbate your molasseslike state. Get the energy moving again! Oxygenate and activate your body through proper deep abdominal breathing, and then you can add fuel to it. Otherwise, you will not only be emotionally depressed, but you will become physically constipated as well. Both are indications you have forced your flow of energy to become stagnant.

An unwanted or complicated pregnancy creates emotional duress in the mother. The fetus and the mother can irritate one another's health. In these cases if the fetus is carried full-term, tissue salts can be helpful, as they aid in transforming the total health state of the mother to a higher level, and do the same for the baby as well. Otherwise, if the mother is unwillingly pregnant, the fetus's consciousness must not only create the new body, but also defend itself from its mother, using energy to fight rejection. In other words, if something eats the mother, it will also eat the fetus because the fetus has little defense against it. It is too busy making the body. The fetus can sense rejection. And depending upon how it perceives its mother in relation to the rest of its environment and experiences, these perceptions will be recorded in its subconscious and affect its total health and relationships through its entire life.

So I cannot simply say, If you are pregnant eat this and don't eat that. That misinformation would burden expectant mothers. Though the mother and fetus have basic nutritional needs, the real nutritional task is for the mother to supply the electropotentials necessary to activate whatever molecular substances are in her body. Then the inherent capacity of her baby's consciousness, which is active the moment the sperm and egg merge, will be able to build a good body from these charged, activated substances. But the body really starts becoming receptive to the direction-giving energy of the consciousness when the brain becomes sufficiently developed to process that information and direct it with the genetic programming of DNA and RNA.

Developing Attunement

The resonance factor, described earlier, applies intimately to the mother and fetus. If the mother is not radiant, the fetus cannot receive. The integration, synergy, and communication between the mother and fetus is an aspect of resonance, the amplitude of which depends upon the mother's total health. If there is little radiance, rather than an integration and synergistic exchange of energies, there is merely a low-level exchange of molecules taking place and no other appropriate processes. There is little vitality. The growth of the fetus is a bland, chemical process with little emotional energy in motion or radiant attachment involved, which is so vital in comforting the baby's consciousness. Maternal resonance allows the child to become a more radiant, actualized person even while in the womb. That can make a tremendous difference in the entire life of the child! There are opportunities present in each stage of life which are hard to duplicate in any other stage, especially those of the prenatal stage.

Radiant electropotentials maintain the processes of attunement between the mother and fetus. It is essential that the mother keep her body moving and energized with such activities as walking, swimming, or yoga. These activities will add to her receptivity to the fetus. Mental exercises include appropriate perceptualizations of the gestating body. The idea is not to put a specific form there, as it is possible to impede the baby's own forming processes, but to perceive the womb environment as ideal, as nurturing, one which allows full and perfect development of the senses and a form compatible with the baby's consciousness. The mother will be able to pass that perception on to the baby.

Another way to help create a receptive environment is for both parents to read to the fetus with sincere intonation. It will be able to perceive its parents' sincerity and love. Parents can also communicate through music and color. They can affect the fetus indirectly by the moods these types of energies create in the mother, as well as directly by the effect the energies have upon the fetus. Red, for example, will vitalize the mother and fetus. Green will cool them down and preserve the life active in the womb.

Music functions in much the same way. If parents play music with many distortions in it, the child will desire and resonate with distortions later in life. If music is played to satisfy a need of the mother, it will meet a need of the child, whether it is a need to be stimulated, activated, released, stabilized, or even decelerated. Whatever is a need of the mother, be it a physical, mental, emotional, or nutritional need, it will also be a need of the baby, because the baby is totally dependent upon the mother for functional materials.

Ideally, couples strive to be in the best total health state possible before conception, knowing that their dynamically receptive environment and their love for one another will be transferred to the fetus. It is beneficial for both wife and husband to train themselves to consciously direct the forms and functions of their bodies. The ability to voluntarily control the body can be realized through meditation, proper nutrition, autogenics, breathing regulation, visualization, and nonattachment (unconditional expression). Such techniques will not only enhance the couple's health, but the ability to self-regulate can also be transferred to the fetus.

Another factor has a significant impact on the parents' health and consciousness, as well as on fetal development: belief systems. Belief systems are secondhand information that comes from an outside authority, and are one of the greatest causes of ill health and disharmony today! Living according to beliefs parallels being in the low-amplitude beta state.

If the parents are seeking to replace belief systems with knowing systems, they might make changes in their way of life, perceptions, and concepts. During gestation the fetus partakes in these processes too, and benefits from the dynamics of its parents' changes. Changing from belief systems to knowing systems can be difficult for the parents, at least in the beginning, as they become more self-individualized. Such transition periods and behavior changes have a tremendous effect upon a person's nutritional state and nutritional needs. As mentioned before, changes in states of health and consciousness can be accompanied by changes in diet in order to physically activate and express them. These changes are based upon knowingness, self-actualization, and full realization of individual potentials through experiential living—what an environment for parents to provide for their developing child!

The physical health of every person is predominantly based upon what happens in the nine months of gestation. The purpose of the consciousness of each developing fetus is to sculpture the body. The fetus's consciousness does not provide material for the body. Instead, it is the sculptor of the body. The consciousness of the fetus can be the most expanded and developed possible, but if it does not have the materials the body will not take the form necessary to fully express its consciousness. Or if it has the materials necessary but there is constant interference in the processes from family belief systems, there will also be impairment of the sculpturing process.

The womb and the relationship of the parents with one another and with the fetus set the basis for the physical, mental, and emotional health of the child. In most cases the child will have a difficult time making changes afterward. But it can be done. All things which occurred in the prenatal state can be transcended.

Some behavior of parents impedes their infants in their developing knowing systems. In what ways do parents do this? Aside from not living by knowing systems themselves, they weigh their babies. They measure them. They judge them based upon how long they have been alive. From these statistics they discern that they do not have the capacity to act upon their potentials. That is their first mistake. For instance, infants know how to survive, but parents wait until they are at least two or three years of age before "teaching" them how to swim. Well, children know how to swim from birth, but the parents transfer their thought patterns and expressions to the children. They believe that because they are small and only one day old, or one week old, or one year old that they can't do that. This is impressed upon the child's subconscious, which regulates the body and processes new information by comparing it with what has previously been encoded.

Parents do not do this just with swimming. They do this with everything! Ultimately, the child rarely gets a chance to express her potentials, possibly unless an accident happens during that time. Then the child's spontaneous behavior or survival response will clash with the family's belief system, which says, It's impossible that a child could have known how to do that. It's a miracle. Such statements deny the child's potentials.

Whether before or after birth, the younger the child, the more susceptible that child is to the nature and character of the environment. Though the fetus is highly adaptable, it is also highly influenced by its environment throughout gestation. A growing body of progressive research strongly suggests that the fetus's consciousness is able to perceive everything in detail as it happens in the outer environment. Once the baby is born, the brain and body play back tapes of what occurred during the prenatal state. During gestation the fetus cannot say to its parents, "Hey, cut it out! Quit fighting with each other. I am busy making a body." Or, "Quit telling me I have to be a boy! I am already making a girl." It can only record these scenes, and once the baby is born, the tapes are played back whenever a similar situation occurs, such as parental resentment toward one another or the child, reinforcing their effect. These tapes are played back in their totality. There is no chance for editing. The editing should have taken place during the taping; it cannot take place during playback.

After birth, the child becomes a participant in the family belief systems. Depending upon the family and the degree to which the child accepts its beliefs, the child will modify his behavior, and thus his ability to respond to life situations will be limited. Choices become narrowed because the child's expression of his potentials and uniqueness has been restricted. If parents become aware of the effects of belief systems on their child, they will realize he is not developing in his totality. Their belief systems are not valid for the child, because the child has not tested them. Development and lack of development of potentials affect physiological development and glandular activity, as well as mental and emotional maturity.

As I stated earlier in this chapter, science accepts that most children from birth until around seven years of age are in a predominantly delta/theta brain wave state. During that time we say they lack the ability to reason, which is true not only because of being predominantly in delta/theta, but also because reason is not expected of them. The predominance of delta/theta allows them to be very sensitive to what is happening in their environments. They will interpret this information and act upon it in accordance with the actualization and activation of their potentials and the influence of the family belief systems.

To assure their children's health and happiness, parents must consider each child as an individual. Parents can do this by observing, rather than intervening and bringing the child back in line with their expectations of what the child could be and how he could behave. For example, the father may see his son becoming a top athlete. The child may have that potential, and he may also have a tremendous mental capacity. In the early years the boy may already be grabbing mental information from a variety of sources. If he would be encouraged by the family, these sources would allow him to develop a brain and body more capable of expressing both the athletic and mental stimulation which he would be attracting through his resonance. By the father observing and nurturing his son, rather than directing him, father and son would enjoy one another, and be in peace and health. The boy's diet would reflect this mind–body harmony as he chose types and quantities of food which would enable him to put his potentials into action.

If the child is more attracted to mental development than physical development, then food requirements will be more oriented toward "mental nutrition." This is a nutrition that feeds the activation of mental potentials more than physical potentials, but the child's mental and physiological needs are still synchronized. Mental nutrition is not only an allegory. It is more than exposing a child to new thoughts, music, art, nature, or creative expression, though these are all types of mental nourishing. A child whose first function is to become a scholar needs different biochemical nutrients than, for example, the child whose first function is to become an athlete.

But this is where we sometimes miss an important aspect of nutrition. We recognize that people who spend most of their time studying eat less and eat differently than people who are totally physically involved. But physically oriented people need to also nourish and express mental capacities. If only physical involvement is nourished and encouraged by a child's parents, mental development is neglected, thus limiting the child, narrowing her life. Stagnation and ill health will result. When parents combine observing their children with their quest of personal fulfillment, they will not try to live through their children, nor will the children need to try to live for their parents. It is not through giving the child "everything I didn't have" that parents help children see life as a source of wonder and enrichment, but rather by challenging one another in a living way, rather than in an authoritorian or rebellious way.

So there is a need for different predominant types of nutrition. These depend upon what the person as a child, adolescent, and adult experiences and needs to express through life's stages. Ideally nutritional programs would nourish both physical and mental potentials in a synergistic way, so when a person needed to make changes, he would not be dominated by one aspect of his personality. Each person should develop as many of his potentials as possible, rather than specializing at the expense of everything else.

We should become well-rounded individuals, with the well-roundedness being a product of our uniquenesses. When a person specializes it can be hard to make changes. An athlete being forced to retire from her sport, a professional soldier retiring from the service, a homemaker watching her last child leave home, are examples of people who may be unprepared to usher in change. They may crave the familiar, but they can no longer have it. Or they may have other urges, but not the energy to put those urges into action. It is sad to see someone go downhill not because she got old, but because she was unprepared to enjoy new forms of expression. Every activity will be more fulfilling when you know you have the potential to accommodate change.

When parents start to discover potentials in their children during early childhood, they can help them develop those without questioning what eventually will become of them. A child may have an interest for a day, and then drop it. The child's health and self-expression will be much better if the parents allow him to drop it, as it is of no further use. Children should not be forced to carry things they do not want, or they will not be able to do what they could.

The best thing parents can do for their children during childhood is prepare them to handle the onslaughts of social belief systems and peer pressure awaiting them at school. As I mentioned in the beginning of this chapter, children seven to thirteen are predominantly in the alpha brain wave state. Alpha works with the subconscious, which regulates physiological processes such as heart rate. It also processes new information and compares it to belief systems, complexes, phobias, or affirmations which may have developed during the prenatal state and early childhood. The body, as the vehicle of expression, is still undergoing rapid growth. The glands are developing so that they will enable the body to express the child's mental and emotional states. In other words, assuming there was a proper prenatal development, the body is adapting itself to express the child's state of consciousness. Influence pressed upon the child during this time can have profound effects. These can range from enabling her to be a fully functional individual to stifling her through impeding physiological growth and hindering mental and emotional progress. Nutrition, impression, and expression are the basic variables which affect each person's development.

Effects of Social Imprinting

Important changes and expectations begin to occur around the age of seven, as children become involved in the societal belief systems taught at school. From that age on they are directed toward reason (which is the ability to form judgments and draw conclusions) and rationale (which is the ability to explain reasoning). They are directed to conform to society's belief systems. Each person is judged on how well he reflects society. If the child's mind and body are weak, he is susceptible to becoming a product of society, rather than a product of his own potentials. How susceptible the child is to becoming merely a product of society depends upon his immune capacity, as determined by his health and consciousness. This is why the parents' nurturing of the child's potentials is vital if we are to have a society of free-thinking, expressive, creative individuals, rather than social clones. Helping children flourish is a challenging opportunity for parents! It requires that parents continuously express themselves.

The word *education* means "to bring forth." Unfortunately, family, school, and society usually engage in social training rather than educating. Children start school while they are in a sensitive alpha state, a level of awareness which is usually different from that of their parents and teachers. Because the alpha state works with the subconscious, children are susceptible to suggestion. While in school they are actually prompted to register every impression they get from society, and then play it back for a reward. This is an effective method of social training, but a poor method of educating. It brings forth little unique expression. What potentials are brought forth are ones outside authorities would judge to have value. They offer rewards based upon that expression. This reward and punishment system of education makes a strong impression on children, and modifies their behavior according to how well they have become members or reflections of society.

This system can undo everything parents have done to bring forth their child's potentials during gestation, infancy, and early childhood. The structure and physiology of the child's body will start to change. It will demand certain nutrients in order to adapt itself to expressing new impressions. These impressions will continue to affect behavior throughout life, as what is recorded by the subconscious interprets, catalogs, measures, files, and expresses every influence, then compares it with how well it fits what has already been recorded, thereby, over time, obliterating spontaneity—and obliterating health.

Later in life, say from the midthirties until death, people can go through real structural stress as they try to undo the processes which have created their physical, mental, and emotional states and social relationships. It's a risk to shed belief systems. It's a risk to replace them with knowing systems. And to make those changes, the body has to be prepared to express the change in health and consciousness. How much better it would be to establish an optimal state of being at the start! To do this, parents first need to build their children's immunity. Then they will be able to contribute to society in a much greater way.

Physical, mental, and emotional development is affected as children are indoctrinated into being reasonable and rational reflections of society. Of course, we need to express reason and rationale, but we have specialized in being reasonable and rational. That is the problem. That is why, by the age of thirteen, we are in a predominantly beta brain wave state. Beta is ordinarily a state of low amplitude and low frequency. Being in beta is like listening to a radio station that has little power and little information—when we could be listening to the satellite news!

And how do we tune into and decode the satellite news? By expressing our total beingness, which creates integration and communication between the different beta states. It also synchronizes both hemispheres of the brain. When in delta, the state of mind–body harmony, our bodies are best able to rest and repair themselves, because there is little mental or emotional interference. We have appropriately expressed everything. The theta state is our intuitive information source, our satellite news network. The alpha state interprets that information according to the impressions registered in the subconscious memory and then, through beta, we are able to verbalize it, express it, make that information available to others. This type of beta state is high-powered. It has a relatively high amplitude and frequency. It is powerful enough to cut through the static of the local stations. We can not only hear, but we can also be heard. We can express ourselves through the vehicle of the body.

If a person uses the different brain wave states, which are actually different levels of consciousness, she will spontaneously become quite articulate at age thirteen. Belief systems in that individual will diminish, and she will live according to her own knowing and interpretation of firsthand information. Because of this the glands and hormones will function at a greater level of activity.

The purpose of the thymus and lymphatic system, for example, is to make your garden bloom, to seed it, protect it, fertilize it, and allow it to mature, rather than fighting pests and weeds, which are toxins created by stagnation. When the lymphatic system is free to do its gardening, your potentials and insights come to fruition. That generates greater resistance. That is how radiance is attained. You will not have to put energy into building fences around your garden to keep it from being trampled, because your level of consciousness is the fence itself, a high-powered electrical fence! You will not have to use chemicals to kill pests and weeds, because the current around your garden will not allow anything of a lower nature to enter. Only those who have a compatible voltage can enter, and they will respect that garden, adding to its beauty.

But, for most children, the usual indoctrination process occurs, for most adults in authority are in a predominantly beta state. Because they must struggle to make their local news heard over the satellite news to which children are tuned, they use the system of reward and punishment to make their jobs easier. Gradually, children tune in more to that than to their own satellite news network. This relates back to Chapter 1 and the discussion on the crystal nature of the human body, which is so important in communication. All the pressures put upon children alter their crystalline structures, thereby altering that to which they are receptive.

Chapter 1 also discussed the impact humans are having upon the Earth's environment, especially the increases in radiation and electromagnetism. Those influences are perceived by the fetus. The fetus's energy adapts to these greater energy influences, influences which its parents were not subjected to during their gestation. Logically, the frequencies in which that fetus's energy operates are adapted to that higher state of motion of environmental energy, because where does it get its energy in the first place? In addition to creating its beingness from the mother and father, the fetus takes its energy from the environment. The generation gap is caused as much by differences in energy levels, beliefs, and brain wave states as by anything else.

For example, our ancestors got news from people walking through town. They had the potential to get information by light or radio waves, but the belief systems of the time did not include that, so consequently mental and physical development did not include it. Today, because of the rapid changes in technology and an environment with energy of a different frequency and greater amplitude than before, we see children we describe as hyperactive. But they are merely responding to and embodying the increase in radiation in our Earth's physical environment. They are affected by its electromagnetic changes, changes which have driven them into an energy state different from ours. Therefore, our children are not hyperactive. Rather, in comparison with them, we are hypoactive.

Because of these changes in the Earth, children are more sensitive to and partake of a more universal environment, one which has immediate communication with all aspects of itself, because it communicates through light. This is evolutionary transformation. We are developing a totally different understanding of the universe. As we apply these new principles of understanding we speed up. And if we hold back our children, we will impede their mental development. The more information we receive from satellite news stations, the easier it becomes to be continuously nourished by what is going on within a much greater area. Gradually our minds will become more directed to that expansion and we will be driven into different brain wave states, because our physiological states will be of greater electromagnetic amplitude. Each person's physiological state will become more excited as it matches the nature of the information which the person is perceiving. That will drive the brain to that level of brain wave state in which consciousness starts to expand.

We need to prepare ourselves to receive light-based information and act upon it. There is more to the world than local news, just as there is more to human consciousness than the beta state. The difference between being predominantly in beta and being predominantly in theta is the difference between trying to cut through a steel door with a candle and cutting through it with a laser beam. Theta offers infinitely more power and information.

That is what we can understand about our children. They have adapted to an environment which we created, but of which we ourselves have not fully partaken. They are not in a better state or a worse state than we are, merely a different state. We are hypoactive compared with them, and they are hyperactive compared with us. We are hanging onto the past more than they are. Evolution really has to do with the present and future, not the past. Hanging onto the past forces the evolutionary process to stagnate.

Formal education lags behind evolution. On many of the glandular maps used to teach high school students about the endocrine system, the thymus and pineal are often not included. Yet it is clear to researchers who have extensively studied the immune system that the immune system's effectiveness depends upon the thymus, which has a close relationship with all the other glands. In the more metaphysical sense, the thymus is considered the heart center, or heart chakra, which deals with levels of consciousness. That part of the body has traditionally been seen as the center of a person's beingness, where dense matter is made more refined, and refined matter is made more dense, in order to become physical reality. In other words, energy is continuously transformed from light to fire and back to light.

Scientists know that the immune system operates physiologically in terms of T-cell production, that support cells are produced, and that the spleen is involved. What has been largely overlooked, however, is how a person's level of consciousness, or mental state, affects not only the immune system but the functionality of the rest of the organs as well. One of the best books available on consciousness and the immune system is *The Body Is the Hero*, by Ronald J. Glasser, M.D. (New York: Random House, 1976). Glasser includes several chapters about the physiology of the body's immune system. In his final chapter he discusses the mental state and how it affects all of the body's defenses.

So, with such information available, why are the thymus and pineal missing from some glandular maps? Because, in most cases, these organs have ceased to develop by the age of thirteen or so, and the majority of scientists and doctors consider them to be vestigal organs, organs which were important either in the earlier development of the species or the individual, but are no longer important to the adult. So the pineal just hangs there like a dried pea between the two hemispheres of the brain. It's as though when God finished you off, he thought, Well, let me put something in there. It will never do anything for you, but something should go there. Maybe it will be called the third eye. Of course, in His infinite wisdom, He gave us other organs, such as the appendix and tonsils, which do nothing except get diseased. Only after several million of them have been removed have we begun to think that maybe these organs have functions, but that we simply do not use them.

What could be the purpose of the thymus and pineal such that they do develop in the early years? As with all other organs, they develop and function according to the child's level of consciousness, a level of consciousness which is affected by belief systems, knowing systems, and maturity. Though the child is in the receptive alpha state, he is still influenced by the theta state, and this dilutes the effect of family and social beliefs. The child still has the freedom to develop his own consciousness. He is spontaneous. Reason and rationale are not sufficiently developed that they cause a state that stops these organs from functioning. Consequently, the thymus and pineal develop until about the age of thirteen, when outside influences have sufficiently prepared the child to assume certain social roles and concepts. The child sees these roles in action in society. The development and activity of the endocrine system, which is so important in terms of energy and body regulation, will reflect his state of consciousness and health.

Children are taught a peculiarly Western form of behavior: Don't do anything in life before thinking about it. And, for God's sake, don't do anything unless you know in advance what you are going to get out of it, and then you had better think about it a little longer. Sleep on it. We do not teach children how to think. We teach them how to question! We teach them to take problems to bed with them! No wonder more children are becoming arthritic and insomniac. Stifling their spontaneity and creative expression decreases the quality of their reception of the satellite news.

So, of course, the pineal atrophies. This is the organ responsible for modifying communications, the organ which, metaphorically, transforms communications from 220 volts to 12 volts, so the body can interpret and act upon them. Spontaneity drops, radiance drops, immunity drops. It is that simple.

The thymus seemingly atrophies too, as it reflects this new lower level of consciousness. Consciousness becomes so modeled and behavior becomes so structured that there seems to be no need for those organs to maintain their growing processes. Actually, there is a need, but the need is denied because of belief systems, and the organs function according to those beliefs. They do not maintain an optimal size based upon growth and function. With this lower level of consciousness and hormonal activity, it is more difficult for the child to mature mentally and emotionally. We put tremendous emphasis on physical development and social roles, which accounts for children becoming sexually mature at an earlier age than ever, but they have a reduced mental and emotional capacity to handle their sexuality.

The challenge for parents and teachers is to help children maintain their spontaneity as they learn to use the beliefs and knowingness of others as guides, rather than dogma. Adopting belief systems diminishes our experiential interest and our wanting to know more, because belief systems are absolute. People with beliefs tend to say, "This is the way it is," rather than, "This is the way I perceive it to be."

What we have done is develop a type of reason and rationale which forces us to follow the beliefs of society. We have not developed a reason and rationale which we can use to translate our spontaneity and our intuition to produce something different from what is found in or accepted by society. But it is unnecessary to contradict or berate the belief systems of others. We can use what has been discovered by others to transcend earlier limits or get a new interpretation of what is. If we could accomplish that, even if we are in a predominantly alpha/beta brain wave state, the thymus, the pineal, and the parts of the brain responsible for processing subconscious information would function better, and the entire body would be closer to its natural radiant state of health. Consequently, we would not see these organs shirk their duties after the age of thirteen. They would maintain the size and activity needed for a level of consciousness which first regulates insight, creativity, and spontaneous articulation, said to be right brain activities, while enabling the left side of the brain to use reason and rationale to interpret and articulate that information, that satellite news. This type of reason and rationale is also capable of processing society's belief systems and comparing them with what is known. Then we could say, "Well, this might be okay for society, but it does not fit with my experience and interpretation. So I am going to act upon what I know."

There is no need to deny someone else her belief systems. There is the obligation for each person to act upon what she has discovered. Living according to personal knowing systems is not social rebellion. It is not a recalcitrant state. It is a nourishing way to live and an acknowledgment of one's own interpretation of firsthand experience. Spontaneity increases, radiance increases, immunity increases, creating an electrical resistance capacity in the body, so the body is unaffected by the lower-powered belief systems, which are based upon external authority and generate low-amplitude beta.

Your radiance will affect the pineal, located between the two halves of the brain. Medical science is beginning to say, "Hey, the pineal is a very active gland! We're not quite sure what it does, but maybe, just maybe, it secretes serotonin and melatonin." Those are two major hormones! But because they were also found in the intestinal area, scientists had been confused, assuming that that was where they were produced. Scientists have not assumed that about scores of other substances. They did not question why a neuron in the cerebral area was able to activate the spleen, or the liver, or the gonads. They did not question that adrenaline made the heart beat faster, though the adrenals, not the heart, produced it. But scientists are beginning to realize that the pineal produces two important hormones, hormones which have a different function in the intestinal area than they do in the brain.

The hormone melatonin gives color and protection to the skin. Melatonin is also the main substance which activates the testes to produce testosterone, the male hormone, or power hormone. Some athletes have, in order to increase muscle strength and size, injected themselves with testosterone. It would have been better, of course, if they had injected themselves with a higher level of consciousness and had further activated the pineal to produce melatonin, which would have stimulated the production of a higher quality and quantity of testosterone.

The hormone serotonin is both a neurotransmitter and neuroinhibitor; it helps the brain make sense of and give direction to thoughts. But where can the thoughts be directed if a person's consciousness operates only by belief systems provided by family and society? If such is the case, serotonin will give reason and rationale only to set mental patterns. There will be little capacity for discovery.

You may have heard perhaps the apocryphal story of the woman who always cut the end off the ham and discarded it before she put the rest of the ham in the oven to bake. The first time her husband saw her do that, he asked her why. She said, "Because that's the way my mother did it." So the husband went to his mother-in-law and asked her why she cut the end off the ham. She answered, "Because that's the way *my* mother did it." So the husband went to his grandmother-in-law, who said, "The reason I cut the end off the ham is because I didn't have a roasting pan big enough for the whole thing." That woman operated on a knowing system. Her daughter and granddaughter operated on a belief system; they never directed themselves to discovery.

With a sense of discovery gone, a person does not have to have the courage to change. So the pineal actually produces a serotonin which reflects the level of consciousness. It produces an old guard serotonin, which assures the old patterns stay in place. Any thought which does not agree with the old patterns is not acted upon. In that case the pineal does not function at its full capacity, because the person is not creating an ever-growing reason and rationale based upon interpreting that which he experiences. Rather than know, he chooses to copy. The result is that there is no need to activate the pineal to produce a greater quantity of high-quality serotonin to regulate a new state of reason. Adopting a belief system is like the athlete injecting himself with testosterone—why make your own when you can get it from the outside?

As we do with serotonin, so we do with testosterone, insulin, estrogen, and many other hormones. Not enough there in the body to be functional? No problem, no need to activate the body, no need to change the mental or emotional state, just take this shot, then swallow this pill. But there are problems! The body is not doing its job. It is not assuming responsibility. Simply dumping things into it is not going to stimulate the body to take control! Empower yourself!

Another problem is that most dosages are given in a trial-and-error fashion, and here is where the qualitative aspect comes in. Most hormones are supposed to be secreted by need over a specific period of time. The organs and hormones create a nice balance between need and response. If a person is kept on hormone supplements, it can create a situation where the brain and other organs get confused about what they are responding to. In time the body can become overwhelmed by its own hormones or synthetic hormones. Either can become toxic to the body. In this situation the body is driven from time-released secretion to having to excrete excess hormones.

Excretion occurs because the organ cannot control itself. It is the difference between irrigation and inundation. The quality of the water which irrigates and helps plants grow is no different from that of the water which inundates and drowns. Irrigation is time-released according to need and distributed in the appropriate way. The qualitative difference between irrigation and inundation is the difference in the effect specific amounts of water have upon the plants. The qualitative difference between secretion and excretion is the difference in the effect specific amounts of hormones have upon the mental, physical, and emotional states of each person.

When a person reaches a higher state of consciousness, she constantly gets information from beyond belief systems. She draws in more electropotentials, which are mostly drawn in by the pineal. The pineal is sensitive to light. It is similar to the eyes in composition and in nutritional needs. And because science now says all information comes as light, it makes sense that the pineal can process light. The pineal is like a cathode ray tube. It receives and transmits information to and from other parts of the brain so that information can be interpreted.

With an active pineal a person goes from being tuned into the local news–belief system station to being tuned into the satellite news–knowing system station. She is tuned into a more expanded spectrum of knowing. The pineal becomes more activated, because it is transmitting higher-voltage, lower-frequency information. When a person acts upon this information, she gets excited and fully involved in what she is doing, in seeing her efforts take form in the world. So logically, she attains a greater expansion of energy. The more she radiates, the higher the level of health, energy, and information she attracts. But for spontaneous articulation she needs appropriately produced serotonin to give that articulation reason and rationale, or appropriate direction. Otherwise, that new reason and rationale is going to be in conflict with the reason and rationale of a different system, the old, beta-based system, which compares everything with established patterns and beliefs. Old patterns can be transcended only by involvement.

As the pineal changes so that it becomes capable of receiving and transmitting greater energies, and the lymphatic system begins to nurture the garden, rather than fight weeds, then the rest of the body, the vehicle of expression, will also change. To maintain health a person needs to continuously challenge each organ to produce its ultimate state of function in order for that person to fulfill his purpose. This will affect his food intake, because he is beginning to change his vehicle from being one that runs on regular gas and putts around at slow speeds in city traffic to being a race car that runs on high-octane fuel. Ultimately, a person can run on rocket fuel. Function is affected by the relationship between vehicle and fuel, that is, between body and food.

Why do the pineal and thymus normally cease to develop by the age of thirteen? Because the reason and rationale of adolescents are not directed toward individual expression of potentials, but rather what to have in the future. When we are born we want to be. Over time we become aware that being also means having to have something. Let us put those two words together: *be-have*, or *behave*. By the age of thirteen our be-havior is dominated by what we have and that with which we identify.

. So adolescents enter a new state. They go from a state of becoming to a state of behaving. Becoming is a process of movement which has to be activated by the individual. To become, energy must be put into motion; it is emotional to become. To be and to come you need constant activity, that is, expression and experience. But rather than becoming, what do we do? We get. A man has to get that job, in order to get that mansion and that Ferrari, in order to get that wife, who has gotten that money from her parents. A woman has to get a husband who has gotten through behaving. Because of the changing roles of women in our society, women are now attracting diseases which formerly affected only men, for women are now involved with getting in the workplace. They are surprised they haven't become what they wanted. Can you feel the wear and tear behaving puts on the body? The universe is for-giving, not for-getting.

There is nothing wrong with getting, unless you hold onto what you have gotten. But if you put your beingness into getting, it becomes be-getting. *Begetting* means "to give birth." It means as soon as you get something, you let go of it or hold it for only as long as you need it in that form, and then transform it to create something else. You give birth to a new idea. You give birth to an expression. Holding onto it causes the energy to stagnate and causes health problems. You can transform your holding the same way you transform your getting: you put your beingness into it. Then holding becomes beholding. And you say, Lo! Behold! A new birth!

The result of getting is that consciousness is modeled by social standards and beliefs. How does society say you can best succeed? Not by action and not by giving birth, but by getting and holding. But to maintain health it is vital to discover your potentials and to become them. Put yourself in situations in which you must expand your potentials and give birth through them.

If you become something that you are not potentially directed to be, whether because of belief systems, family pressures, economic security, or some other reason, you force your body to malfunction. You force your consciousness to function in a way that is not its intended purpose. This forces your consciousness to stagnate, as well as your reason and rationale. To become a corporate executive when you would prefer to be a river guide, or to become a river guide when you would prefer to be a corporate executive, forces your energy and evolution to stagnate.

To become, you need to know your potentials and pursue their fulfillment. Without that knowing and action, you suffer a loss of courage and happiness. You do not become the expression of your consciousness. You eat food that maintains you in a forced function, which forces your body and consciousness into directions antagonistic to the core of your being. You force-feed yourself. It is like the Christmas goose, which would like to be flying south for the winter but cannot, for people keep stuffing grain down its throat—to get it fat for their dinner.

From approximately eighteen to thirty years of age, people can start to practice and implement the directions of their beliefs and consciousness. Those who act upon their potentials and continuously become what they desire to be, even if their family, peers, and society disagree, will be much healthier than those who do not accept the joy of their potentials. They will perform at much higher levels in whatever they do, because they have their heart and soul in what they do. These people do not count their rewards by numbers. They count their rewards by their happiness, their joy, and their state of excitement. Their excitement is not so much in seeing if they can win over someone else, but in challenging themselves. They risk!

Between the ages of eighteen and thirty, people still have many chances to make changes. What can young adults do to enhance their health and personal expression? They can go on a path of self-discovery and thus not become one-sided. They can explore their desires, and their sources of joy, and become well-rounded people, physically, mentally, and emotionally. Rather than holding onto accomplishments, they can develop great freedom and can use it to pursue potentials felt but as yet unexpressed. This is possible because in most cases the responsibility to parents has been reduced, and commitments to a mate and children have not yet been made.

So there is much freedom of choice. This freedom of adulthood can be powerful when combined with knowing systems, health and radiance, and the privileges of being an adult. During childhood parents can help prepare their children to assume the joys and responsibilities of such freedom.

It can be difficult for young adults, who usually have not yet established families and often do have personal freedom, courage, and initiative, to go on paths of personal discovery. The difficulties for middle-aged adults, who often have been stuck in beliefs for a long time, are even greater. These people think they do not have the capacity to ever get their potentials going, that is, if they think about it at all!

Relationships have a tremendous impact upon expression. For many, their relationships oppress them because, in spite of their belief systems, there is an undeniable knowingness within them which says, "I have not become what I needed." It eats at them. This is why many suffer hypertension, heart disease, and stomach and intestinal problems. Ask them why they do not change their situations and they say, "Well, I have a family to support and bills to pay, so I have to work. I have to behave." And it is true that once relationships are established, they can be hard to leave.

How can you work with a stifling relationship? One way is to allow your partner to develop her or his potentials too. It is not always necessary to break up relationships in order for people to develop. Learn to give each other the freedom to be and to become. Support each other on your paths of discovery. At one point you might be the one who needs to become. At another point it might be your mate who needs to become. Or you may need to become simultaneously, and you can support each other in your individual quests. This can be a stimulating model for your children. They can observe and experience how you, their parents, are both exploring and expanding your potentials and consciousness, yet still maintaining a sharing, caring relationship with each other. The children may come to realize they can explore their potentials too, for you have not made them dependent upon set beliefs. You are not holding onto beliefs any longer. You and your children will have a much greater freedom and will be healthier because of it.

So for those who feel oppressed by family relationships, I would say that getting away from one another will not necessarily make you happy if you do not learn to activate your potentials. Before you look outside the family life or look for someone who seems to share your beliefs and ideas, you might first look for ways to express yourself as an individual within the family. You may discover that involvement with your partner, mate and children, will lead to your evolvement. The key is to create a family which is mutually supportive. Continuously create a dynamic family environment which reflects and enhances your state of consciousness and health. Do not fear change. Do not use your family and your job as excuses or distractions to avoid personal expression. Do not explode—expand! Otherwise, you will limit the expression of your partner and children as well.

How sad that many people actually plan to wait forty years and agree to spend their energy fulfilling someone else's desires before they set out on that path of self-discovery. For forty years they work to fulfill someone else's expectations of what is best for them. They wait until they retire and the children are gone before they really begin to live for themselves.

Forty years of waiting will not leave the mind and body in a very good state of health, one capable of allowing a person to develop her potentials. Often that person's "golden years" become merely a fulfillment of a new set of beliefs, an escape rather than an exploration.

Health is a reflection of beingness. So how can you expect your mental, emotional, and physical states to be ready for the joys and demands of self-discovery if you have fulfilled belief systems your entire life, have allowed yourself to become prematurely old, have believed that your glands should atrophy and cease to function, and that your heart, liver, intestines, and general metabolism should slow down? Your body runs down because it is forced to operate in ways antagonistic to the purposes for which you were born and to the creations to which you should have given birth.

Your conception of aging is like anything else in which you believe—you embody it. You accept as fact that as you age chronologically, you also need to age physiologically. When a specific things happens within your body, people say, "Well, what do you expect? After all, you are at that age." This denies the ability of your regenerative process, which has the capacity to maintain a high state of transformation and radiance. When you become less radiant, it is not because you became a day older, or an hour older, or a minute older, or a second older, it is because you are not expressing what is really happening within you.

Conceptions are not necessarily perceptions. In most cases conceptions are based upon belief systems and prevailing attitudes, which is the mood you project inwardly and outwardly. So you tell people whose behavior you do not like, "Change your attitude." That means, "Change your concept." Fine. But with what can it be replaced? Another concept? Usually. Usually it is replaced with another belief-based concept, which reflects a new association with an outside authority.

Perceptions, which are based upon sensory experience and knowing, should precede conceptions. You express yourself and through that you change your attitudes. In other words, you do not change your attitudes in order to get a better perception, you get a better perception in order to change your attitudes. To do that you have to transcend the concepts under which you have lived. It is not a matter of denying or erasing them. There needs to be a continual process whereby perceptions form conceptions, rather than belief systems forming conceptions. Concepts should be based upon what you are perceiving now and relating those perceptions to what you have already experienced. The experiences you have and the potentials you activate are mainly determined by your belief and knowing systems and attitudes. So changing your perceptions will also change the types of experiences you have. Transcendence is what keeps the universe healthy, and it will keep you healthy too.

For example, the American concept of healthy eating is that a person should eat three meals a day. This is considered to be using the stomach in the appropriate way; the stomach should be healthy. Several years ago a radiologist proposed that because for years I had eaten only two or three very small meals a week, I must have a terribly small, shrunken stomach. He asked me if he could X ray my stomach. He took eighteen X rays, and then compared them with X rays he had taken over the years of other people's stomachs. He found that my stomach was larger than anyone else's. Now, there may be many people walking around the world with larger stomaches than mine, but it was not so much the size which impressed him, it was its appearance. It did not have the appearance of an overused or abused stomach. It occurred to him that my stomach had never been overfilled. Overused stomachs look like a balloon that has been overinflated then deflated. They are shriveled and shrunken, because they have lost some of their elasticity. Overused stomachs are actually smaller than ones which have not been abused. The radiologist told me my stomach looked like the stomach of a healthy thirty-year-old; I was in my middle fifties at the time.

Initially, the radiologist compared my stomach with his belief system, which said my stomach should look a certain way and should have aged. Aging is more dependent upon your belief systems and the proper use of your organs than it is on the time you have been alive. Nonetheless, I am not going to suggest that to maintain a healthy stomach you should eat only three small meals a week, because if you try to mold yourself to that belief, you could make your stomach, and everything else you have, malfunction.

The point is that our concepts of aging and health are based upon what society tells us, rather than on our perceptions and experience. "As a man thinks, so he is." Aging and premature aging occur because the body has not been allowed to function according to its capacity and the purposes of the person.

During a lifetime the body certainly undergoes wear and tear. As you grow, mature, and express your potentials, you experience wear and tear. Premature aging occurs when you go beyond wear and tear to abuse. Using the body is much the same as using any other vehicle. Some people drive their cars for twelve years and keep them looking and running brand new. Others drive their cars for twelve months, and by then they are ready for garbage dumps. Essentially the same thing happens with the body. If you use it for something other than for what it was made, do not expect it to last as long as if you had used it and cared for it properly.

Your body is the vehicle of individual expression. If you realize that all of your body is in your mind, and your mind is the driver of your vehicle, you will be able to maintain your body in order to express your function in life. As you mature through expression, your body will adapt itself to your mental and emotional states of consciousness. Your involvement and expression need never stop! They will become joys unto themselves and will maintain and vitalize the body.

Normally, though, the electropotentials of the body begin to noticeably decline at the age of about sixty. Why? Because the body has been treated like a piece of elastic, stretched beyond its capacity to maintain its tone. Any material loses some of its quality through continuous use, but a person who is involved physically, mentally, emotionally, and spiritually will have a longer-lasting elasticity, a longer-lasting radiance, and a longer-lasting capacity to draw in electropotentials. Another reason for the body's loss of resilience is that we expect it to happen, because we have embodied the belief that as we get older we wear down. Collectively, these influences take away the body's luster of youth, and by the age of sixty the body has become much less capable of drawing in, of resonating with, electropotentials, by which it maintains itself.

It does not have to be that way. Certain substances and tissue salts can activate the brain and also the mental state. Those whose electropotentials have declined need to reassert their desire, so they become radiant again. It all comes down to desire, because desire is the activator for the generative process. For people who have no desire to participate in life any longer, the generative system, that is, the gonads, become practically inactive.

And the hormones produced by the gonads can have a powerful impact on the brain, in turn, especially the pineal and pituitary glands. When these hormones are lacking, people simply cannot involve themselves with their potentials or with life in general. They will begin to avoid things, because their desire, their willingness to risk involvement, is greatly reduced. We have taken for granted that this is what happens when we get old. But age is not an excuse for a lack of excitement.

Kinetic power, which is created in the sexual organs, stimulates the brain. When kinetic power is reduced, you become lustless, desireless. Sexuality is involved in everything having to do with relationships. Sexuality and desire are not limited to sexual intercourse. That is a very narrow definition. Sexuality means interrelating with life, interacting with life, having intercourse with life. If you lack lust, you become lackluster, that is, not radiant. How can the brain attract information of an enlightened nature when it is not turned on? It is like your television. You cannot expect to get the news if your set is not turned on.

Your attitudes, perceptions, and conceptions are tremendously important in determining the quality of your life. You can see this in older people who have not lost their lust for life. They truly enjoy being involved. These people realize how nicely activity maintains the body. They do not feel sorry for themselves if they cannot afford to retire, because they are having too much fun going on the way they are. These people have their sets turned on. They know their potentials. They have taken their energy, put it out into the world, and experienced the fruits of their labor, which, in turn, have nourished new seeds of expression. That is a most creative and self-sustaining process.

The work of these people is not oriented toward results or money; it is oriented toward activity. That is the difference between a workaholic and someone who expresses for the sake of expression. A workaholic may be very active mentally, physically, and emotionally, but she is motivated by what she can get in return. This conditional expression is a form of greed. Though she may be driven by a desire for personal or family survival, it is greed nevertheless, and causes premature aging and disease. Desire is based upon spontaneous, creative expression and joy. Greed is dominated by belief systems, fear of risk, fear of change, and conditional expression.

One of the body's greatest attributes is that it enables you to experience multiple dimensions of energy simultaneously. It is an organism for transforming energy into matter and matter back into energy. In other words, it transforms light to fire to light. The major organs are the prime physical centers for this transformation, with the nerves distributing the different qualities of energy in a continuous flow throughout the body. Let us trace how this energy flow operates.

As you become stimulated by a thought, you become aroused. You can imagine this thought-arousal state as an express train of energy running continuously between the brain, especially the pineal and pituitary, and the gonads. This arousal state creates kinetic strength, which is regulated by the metabolism of the liver, pancreas, and spleen. When the pineal is operating optimally and producing proper amounts of serotonin, the serotonin in the abdominal area gives reason and rationale to that kinetic power. It transforms it from a mere body maintenance state to a power capable of expressing higher states of energy and consciousness. The spleen is also a reserve power source for the gonads when they cannot generate enough energy. The spleen is responsible for your "second wind." That sharp pain in your left side after prolonged exertion is your spleen being activated. The spleen gives your gonads a chance to regulate themselves and generate energy again.

As energy moves up from the spleen, the adrenal glands act upon it. When working properly they help transform that energy out of the gut reaction state, or the fight-or-flight state, to one in which spontaneous action is nourished. In other words, the adrenals help maintain that which was aroused and put that energy into motion as physical action. The adrenals are also involved with feelings associated with energy in motion, that is, emotional energy, such as fear, anger, pleasure, and pain. For example, if you are fearful and hold back what you feel, you will feel a physical stagnation in the solar plexus. You are keeping that emotion from being transformed. Either you have to express that emotion, or, in time, the body will show it as a disease, such as an ulcer. To express that emotion appropriately, you need to allow it to be transformed through the thymus, a higher center. Fear can be transformed by facing it competently and being non-attached to the result.

With your energy in motion, the thymus will not have to be concerned with battling the weeds of stagnation. Instead, it can enable you to respond to your potentials. This expands consciousness, and radiance, and resistance, as you become more involved with outward expression, rather than inward stagnation. In this capacity the thymus is where the "above and below" meet and seek union. This transmutation of energies is what expands awareness and consciousness, thereby increasing immunity.

Above the thymus, in the throat, are the thyroid and parathyroid, two glands responsible for regulating the overall rate of metabolism and growth. The effects of their hormones determine whether you are comparatively balanced, hypoactive, or hyperactive. The thyroid is especially important in regulating your ability to express willpower and spontaneity, using the energy prepared by and pulled up from the lower centers. It also regulates the metabolism of your consciousness. Ideally, this center blends the I self with the higher self, resulting in a unique expression of energy.

The pituitary is a marvelous organ. Known as the master gland, it functions as a prism which synthesizes and desynthesizes both biochemical light energies. As energy comes down from the pineal, the pituitary processes and distributes it to other parts of the brain and throughout the body. The pituitary also synthesizes biochemical and light energies as they come up through the body, integrating them once again. In addition to regulating fluids in the body, the pituitary regulates the nervous system through its association with the hypothalamus. It also helps the thyroid make changes necessary to reach the comparative balance between being underactive and overactive.

The information which comes to the pituitary from the pineal is processed according to the subconscious and past sense perceptions, as stored in the area of the brain known as the hippocampus. Conversely, past perceptions and experiences determine the type of information the pituitary sends to the pineal, which affects the quality of information the pineal transmits and with which you resonate.

The pineal is your connection with the transpersonal self and your greatest health/energy state. It transforms light energy in order to make it understandable and usable for you. It is responsible for your being able to transcend into knowingness. But the pineal is never fully functional until all other energy centers and organs are functioning appropriately.

Volumes have been written about what was discussed in the preceding few paragraphs. But the idea I want to share with you is that the body produces and processes more than just physical, biochemical, and electromagnetic energies. Because of its crystalo-colloidal nature, the body is able to produce and process many different forms of energy. Each cell has the potential to produce and transform varying qualities of energy, from subtle to dense, and use them for information, expression, communication, and nourishment.

When you are spontaneous you are nonattached. Energy flows in and expression flows out. You experience the pleasure of seeing what you have accomplished take form in the world. You feel joyful and alive, and you are not eaten by things in the environment.

Unhappiness, hypertension, and a feeling of being stressed out are really caused by feeling incompetent. If you feel incompetent you tend to fight the outside world, rather than use it as an instrument for expression. The world is your partner. When you feel competent you know that no matter how you handle a situation, it will work out fine. The situation is resolved; it becomes solvent again. Then you do not feel tense. You perceive stress as a challenge and an indication that you need to put more energy into your activity, instead of holding back and doubting your ability to deal with it.

If you allow desire to become part of your whole being, the desire will become strong enough that you will want to express it. Remember, expression is a two-way street. Your radiance, which is determined by your expression, then determines what you attract from the universe, including ideas. Ideas are attracted to you and are initially processed through the pineal gland. You need energy to put an idea into form. If your desire to give it form becomes strong enough, that is, you receive it, perceive it, and make a decision to act upon it, you will get more aroused by it.

The pineal will then stimulate the gonads to release more power. The power comes up and activates the glands and energy centers one at a time in order to bring that idea into beingness. Your thoughts actually create your reality, but only if you pay attention to them and get excited about acting upon them. The moment you start paying attention to an idea, the gonads are stimulated and release energy, which eventually stimulates the thyroid into the state necessary to prepare the body to express it, to will it.

Whatever you will is synthesized by the pituitary gland, as determined by your health state, beliefs, knowingness, and past experiences with the final product being sent to the pineal. Then the pineal integrates the amplitude and frequency of that thought with what is flowing into you from the universe. This incoming and outgoing flow of information enables you to expand upon what you have put into the world, so continuous transformation takes place.

Too often we set our potentials aside and put our desires on hold for someone else's apparent sake. We create conflicts whch don't need to exist, either an inner conflict of, Should I or shouldn't I? or an attempt to justify our lack of expression because of what others expect of us. Too often we create a time schedule by which self-expression, if it comes at all, can come only after we have fulfilled all social expectations, only to find that those never end. We need to know what to do now, and then do it, in spite of everything else. Spontaneity is not easy, especially for those of us who have family or obligations incurred by other structured situations. Physiological problems often arise from structured situations. Expectations repress natural spontaneity.

What can you do about it? Simply begin expressing mentally, without any brakes on! Divert your attention from the molasses-like situations of work or of living someone else's belief systems. Begin perceptualizing what you would like to be doing right here and now. There is no need to wait for a better time or for someone's permission. Perceive yourself fully and joyfully involved. Then because you have put it outside of yourself, you become nonattached to the result, and you immediately begin to get more radiant. The result is that time slows down for you. Your work goes faster; you do it practically automatically. You become so involved on one level of expression that the other levels begin to run more smoothly.

It is like a slow-moving river clogged with boulders. The river is your expression, and the boulders are the barriers to your expression. If you had to remove the rocks, it would be very hard to push them out of the channel. You could spend all your time trying to get the rocks out of the channel without getting the river moving. But as soon as the river starts to flow and gains power from the desire to get back to its origin, you will find that you don't need to do anything to the rocks, because the current takes the rocks with it. You do not need to remove the rocks if you keep the current going at all times.

Keep your current moving. Generate new ideas and activity constantly. Do what you enjoy and the barriers to your expression will roll away easily, so easily, in fact, that soon you will not need to pay attention to them. You see, you do not want to take time pushing rocks out on the bank, where they might fall back into the river again.

Know that you can express at any time. Guilt, fear, feelings of incompetence, and the belief that you must stick with it in order to succeed dulls your luster. They keep you from what you love and from health and happiness. People often put too much emphasis on what must be done and what should be done, rather than what could be done. If you understand what you could do, then the "should do" is included and accomplished within what you could do. Then you express not just yourself, but your higher self also.

Outside authorities tell you what you should do. The inside authority, the higher self, tells you what you can do. If you are not in communication with the higher self, your body will become dis-eased, because the energy flow has become stagnant.

The sooner you assume responsibility for developing a knowing system, the sooner you will become aware of what your potentials are. Whatever you do, love it!

Chapter 5

Remedies for Energy Regulation

In regard to self-diagnosis and energy regulation, many people have asked me, "Jack, why don't you say exactly what it is people should take for this symptom or that symptom?"

The answer is that for a particular individual who was displaying certain symptoms, I might advise that person to take a number of specific tissue salts and therapies. The next individual I counseled could have exactly the same symptoms—plus an added one. That added symptom would make the need for supplements and the energies needed to be activated totally different. The entire organism needs to be regulated; none of the organs work in isolation. So you cannot merely say, "Take this for this and that for that."

The body will tell you what it needs. You can learn to understand body language (which is much more than what posture a person assumes) by trusting the wisdom of the body and your own knowingness. If you do not want spaghetti today, it may be not because you had it so many times this week already and so are bored. Maybe you needed it six times, but you simply do not need it now. Hearing what your body says leads to awareness gained through knowing, not logic. You can want to become only what you already are, but you have to become aware of what it is that you are. That is why you have a consciousness and a state of body awareness. If I become nauseated, I should know what the body is trying to tell me. How do I find out? I ask my body. That might sound strange, but you tell the body what to do and the body responds to your commands and your mental and emotional states. It's important to be sensitive to how your body responds to your commands and to the environment; it's important to hear what it is saying. Remember, the body is a marvelous and wise organism. It does not lie.

You can develop that sensitivity through attaining the alpha and meditative states, as explained in my book *Voluntary Controls* (New York: E.P. Dutton, 1978). It helps to know some of the symptoms associated with certain functional deficiencies and excesses. Some symptoms and remedies are described in my book *Human Energy Systems* (New York: E.P. Dutton, 1980); others are discussed in this chapter. These will serve as a primer to your intuition, as well as an introduction to the processes regulating mind and body energies. You are always in a state of transformation, so continuously check the state of your body, use your body as your laboratory to discover what happens to you when you are in a particular mental, emotional, or physical state. Ask yourself how these states affect your nutritional and activity requirements. In this way you develop self-trust.

This chapter contains basic energy regulation principles and self-regulation remedies, and examples of both in action. The tables relating to the tissue salts tell what basic substances and electropotentials are for what organs and what conditions. The tables also explain, for example, that if you have pain under the left side of your ribs, you know that the pain is in your spleen.

The tables further explain that because the function of the spleen is related to the functions of the liver and pancreas, you can safely assume that all three organs are suffering from mineral imbalances. In Appendix B of *Human Energy Systems,* you will see those organs require four main ingredients: chlorine, magnesium, potassium, and sodium. If you take them in homeopathic tissue salts or solutions, you cannot cause yourself harm. You are using electropotentials, which are charged particles with a certain degree of activity, rather than actual molecular substances. If the body does not need those electropotentials, it will not use them. The body will integrate only what it can use. Always keep in mind the need to integrate all functions and energies of the body with one another, as well as with your mental and emotional states and different levels of consciousness, that is, the delta, theta, alpha, and beta states.

Most physical health problems begin in the gastrointestinal area and are due to a lack of proper hygiene for the abdominal organs and poor digestion and assimilation of food. Poor digestion pollutes the intestinal environment, which simultaneously further impedes digestion and destroys the structure of the digestive organs. So in detoxifying the body, the abdomen is the most logical place to start.

Misconceptions about the purpose of food, an imbalanced diet, excessive eating, a less than harmonious mental or emotional state, as well as poor food quality, contribute to intestinal problems. They all lead to the body working too hard, for it is not as healthful and radiant as it could be. The body wears down, bit by bit, organ by organ, and soon it is unable to work at all. In other words, if a person cannot activate energy from food, she will certainly not be able to draw energy from the environment.

People could become more productive and independent through nutritional as well as psychological therapy. Without the proper assimilation of necessary nutrients, the brain cannot direct the body to fulfill the potentials of the mind. But virtually everyone can become significantly stimulated through reestablishing the biochemical balance of their bodies through nutrition.

There are many remedies which can put the tone and efficiency back into the intestinal area. Indeed, a proper individualized diet will maintain that tone and efficiency. But if you have had too many large holiday meals, or too much alcohol, or too many arguments with your boss, or too many bouts with the blues, all of which can slow down your digestive processes, you will have to detoxify your digestive tract so it becomes efficient again, so the brain is properly nourished again, and so the muscles, joints, and lymphatic system become rejuvenated and capable of joyously expressing your being again.

One of the misconceptions people have about detoxifying themselves is that they can merely quit doing whatever they have been doing in excess. They might decide to go on a fast, which more and more people are telling me they do regularly. But fasting won't work for them, because their fasts are unreasonable. They have been gorging themselves for years; suddenly they decide that a three-day or ten-day fast will make their bodies glow again, put their spirits in communion with the highest recesses of the cosmos. It does not work that way. Why? Take a glass of dirty water, for example. Let it sit for ten days, and all the toxins will still be there. Then add to it the purest water you can find. What do you have now? Dirty water. The pure water stirred up all the existing pollutants and was adulterated immediately. Apply that example to the human body, and you will see that you can fast as much as you want, you can eat all the good foods you want, but you will continue to increase the toxicity of your body if your body is too toxic to activate them.

Fasting is not a detoxification process. The most it can do is temporarily halt further toxification. But a fast can also hurt the body, especially if a person plunges into it. Going from heavy eating to no eating is a shock to the body; it damages it more than it helps.

Human Energy Systems suggests a thirty-six day fast, which consists of gradually cutting back on food for twelve days, then abstaining from all food and liquid except water or fruit juice for twelve days, and then gradually resuming food intake over a course of twelve days. Fasting is done only after detoxifying the body and attaining a proper mental–emotional state, that is, a state in which you have attained a certain degree of harmony with your inner and outer environments through involvement with them. You can trust yourself to know when you have attained that state. You put the idea out that you are preparing to fast and then trust yourself to know when a fast will add to your energy, rather than deplete it.

In the meantime you can undertake any of several physical detoxifications. One very fast external one consists of regularly taking Epsom salts baths. An Epsom salts bath does not do anything to the body per se. The body does not absorb the salts. Epsom salts changes the density of the water, thereby causing a greater surface tension, enabling the bath water to draw toxins from the body.

To make the bath most effective, the bathwater has to have a denser salt concentration than the body. I recommend using four to five pounds of Epsom salts in a bathtub full of water as hot as you can take. Stay in there for at least fifteen minutes. The Epsom salts will cause you to become buoyant and hence relaxed in the water. If you get drowsy while in the tub, use an inflatable pillow to rest your head. Many times after soaking you will see a black film around the tub. The film consists of toxins you have released. Follow the bath with a brisk, cold shower, and dry yourself with a rough cotton towel to stimulate your pores, muscles, and nerves.

It is preferable to take the baths at night, so you can go straight to bed afterward. Sometimes after soaking you will have lost so much fluid and toxins that the body loses its resistance. That is a great feeling! It may take all your strength just to fall into bed, but the body can restore itself after a good night's sleep. After such hydrotherapy you will be able to go into a deep delta sleep, the state in which the mind and body are in harmony, the state in which the body restores itself.

After the bath, or a series of baths that you take every other day for a week, you can go on a fast. As you cut down on your food intake and your body becomes less burdened, you will begin to feel very energetic as the body attunes itself to operating on more subtle forms of energy. Of course, there will be a loss of physical strength and endurance initially, but other forms of energy may become more prevalent. You may notice a need for less sleep. Your heart rate may drop substantially. You may have a greater degree of voluntary control over your physical processes and heightened sensory awareness. Following the fast, if you feel the need for food supplements, especially tissue salts, they can be especially helpful in regulating the energy flow of your mind and body.

Another excellent method of physical detoxification is the sulfur bath. Put one to two tablespoons of liquid sulfur into your bathtub of water as hot as you can take, and soak for eight to ten minutes. The sulfur will penetrate through your pores and into your system, particularly where you perspire. Note that those who perspire a great deal under the arms will smell like sulfur dioxide, a smell similar to that of an oil refinery or rotting eggs. That will last a couple of days or so. You can eliminate that sulfur smell by adding a few drops of fragrant oil, such as rose oil, eucalyptus oil, or pine oil to your bathwater.

One of the reasons garlic and onions are so good for you is because they have a high sulfur content, which activates and cleanses. Sulfur stirs up and shifts waste matter, aiding in elimination. After the sulfur does its job, it is up to you to continue the process by rebuilding yourself after the waste materials have been eliminated.

Another method of detoxification is the enema. Ancient Egyptian preventive medicine was based upon the timely use of three things: herbs, emetics, which cause vomiting, and enemas. The coffee enema is one effective enema. It is not coincidence that many people who normally have three to four bowel movements a day drink one cup of strong black coffee about a half an hour after each meal. Coffee stimulates the liver and colon, allowing them to have more frequent and easier bowel movements. The colon is not constantly stagnant and full. Together with a stimulated liver, this gives them better assimilation of nutrients and elimination of toxins.

Of course, the coffee enema is a much faster and more effective tonic than simply drinking coffee. The coffee enema consists of three heaping tablespoons of ground coffee boiled with one quart of water. Let the coffee steep for five to ten minutes, strain the grounds, and allow the coffee to cool to lukewarm, about the temperature of your body's core. Then prepare yourself for a high enema, one which cleans the entire colon as well as stimulates the liver.

The high enema works by gravitation. Take the enema nude while in the bathtub. Get an enema bag with a long hose, and hang the bag from the shower head. Put a little petroleum jelly on the insertion tip, and lie down with your feet upon the edge of the tub or against the wall, so the enema will go as high as possible into the abdominal area. Insert the tip and gravity will pull the fluid into the colon. With the fluid in your system, massage the liver, which is under your lowest right rib, in a rotating motion.

What does the coffee do for the liver? Excessive toxins and a lack of proper nutrition can cause the liver to lose its tone, go lax. The liver is neither contracting nor expanding; it is not responding to the body's needs. It is holding onto toxins, rather than releasing them. The coffee is a stimulant. It startles the liver. The liver wakes up! It releases its toxins. The coffee immediately chelates, or grabs, the toxins, and carries them back off through the colon and out the body. This method is fast and effective.

I always caution against doing anything more than necessary, and most people will need only one to two enemas in a week's time. The second one is only to check out if everything has gone. The second one should run clearer and have less odor. From then on you can take a periodic liver flush to ensure the liver stays clean and functional.

The liver flush consists of two ounces of lemon juice, which is about the amount of juice squeezed from a good-sized lemon. Add to this one teaspoon of olive oil, one teaspoon of blackstrap molasses, a knifepoint of cayenne pepper, and four ounces of lukewarm water. Stir thoroughly and drink all at once. How often should you do a liver flush? It depends. It depends on self-discipline and self-knowingness. If you know you are still not functioning properly, because you lack energy, then maybe you have more toxins which are impeding your energy flow. You will also know that your liver is not functioning properly if you are not having daily bowel movements or movements of a proper consistency.

You can determine your waste's consistency by observing how it lies in relation to the toilet bowl waterline. The first kind is a ship which has only its keel in the water. It is riding too high; all decks are above the waterline. The second one is a ship with only the upper deck above the water. The third is a submarine; it goes straight to the bottom. Of these three, the second is the most satisfactory. It is neither too heavy nor too light. The first is loaded with oxygen, other gases, and nonmetabolized fatty oils, which is why it floats too high. The submarine is loaded with undigested nutrients. There will always be a few submarines, but if you have them consistently, you know it is because you are not metabolizing your nutrients. The liver and colon are not able to do their jobs.

Unfortunately, many people do not appreciate or experience the virtues of regular bowel movements. Few people have two or three movements a day. If I say to a person, "You are consti-pated," that person may answer, "No, I'm not!" So then I ask, "When did you have your last bowel movement?" The answer I get is, "Day before yesterday. I am very regular. I go every two or three days."

It can be hard to talk to such people, because they have a belief stuck in their minds. And not only is this belief stuck in their minds, it is stuck in their bodies as well. For them, being regular means going once every other day. I have observed that healthier people go two to three times a day; they have a lot of directed healthy activity occurring. They are involved and evolving. Some people say if you go more than once a day, too much is leaving the body. My perception is that these people do not have enough activity going on in themselves.

In addition to keeping the intestinal area functional with enemas and liver flushes, you can also try the gallbladder flush, which is much like the liver flush. Mix two ounces of lemon juice, three teaspoons of olive oil, a knifepoint of cayenne pepper, and four ounces of lukewarm water. By omitting the molasses, which nourishes the liver, and including more olive oil, you get a greater response from the gallbladder.

Like your liver, your kidneys are a waste treatment plant. Kidney and bladder problems are almost always related to mineral imbalances caused by the nonassimilation of nutrients. The most frequent kidney and bladder problems are stones and gravel.

The main culprits behind kidney and bladder deposits are nonmetabolized calcium and magnesium. Magnesium deposits are discussed later in this chapter. Apple cider vinegar works marvelously on the calcium deposits. It softens them so they can pass through the urinary tract. You can prove this for yourself with a simple demonstration. Fill a glass with about five ounces of apple cider vinegar. Soak a raw egg in it, shell and all, for twenty-four hours. Then get a soda bottle and fill it three-fourths full with water. Now take the egg out of the apple cider vinegar, and you will find that the eggshell, which is made of calcium, is as soft as the egg itself. You will be able to squeeze the egg, including the shell, through the neck of the soda bottle. As soon as it falls in the water, it hardens again. You can let people guess how you got that whole egg into the bottle.

What does this demonstrate? It shows how apple cider vinegar will work upon stones or gravel, softening them so the body can remove them. If you have a burning sensation when you urinate, that could be from stones or gravel passing through your urinary tract. Drink about four to eight ounces of apple cider vinegar every day for about five days, and that should clear your system. You may dilute the vinegar with two to four ounces of lukewarm water and add a teaspoon of honey to make it more palatable. To maintain the kidneys you can do a kidney flush periodically. The flush consists of two ounces of apple cider vinegar, four ounces of lukewarm water, and one teaspoon of honey. You can alternate the kidney flush with the liver flush, doing one every day for a week or two to tone and clear your filtration systems.

There are many reasons for arthritis, including mineral imbalances. It is especially alarming to see more and more children being crippled by this degenerative disease. There are mental causes of arthritis (there is truth to the statement, "Rigid in mind, rigid in body"), but there are physiological, dietary, and poor-habit causes as well. In this country a major contributor to arthritis is the tremendous amount of citrus fruits and citric acid people ingest. Excessive citric acid is being recognized as a cause of arthritis. Soft drinks, some fruit juices, and canned vegetables are major sources of excessive citric acid.

Why are citrus fruits potentially damaging? Their citric acid dissolves the thin film of oil which lubricates bones and joints. When that oil is gone, calcium in the blood passes over bare bone. That calcium has an affinity for the bones' calcium and, rather than being utilized by the tissues in need of calcium, the calcium settles down upon the bones. Calcium deposits, especially in joints, cause stiffness and pain. To make matters worse, some people with growing calcium deposits take calcium supplements. Much of the calcium they are ingesting already is not being assimilated, so supplements only aggravate the calcium deposits and arthritic condition.

Again, the body needs to be made functional. This is where fish oils come in, especially cod liver oil. Fish oils are excellent sources of vitamins A and D, but they are also the only oils which will relubricate dried bone. When the bones have been relubricated, calcium will again be utilized by the tissues and systems in need of it. Consequently, there will be better movement in the joints, helping blood circulation, and the arthritis will be reduced. Two tissue salts make a powerful team to eliminate calcium deposits and make the calcium functional. Calcium phosphate is a type of phosphoric acid which breaks up the deposits of the joints. Calcium sulfate has distribution properties; it enables the body to distribute calcium to where it is needed and excrete the excess calcium.

Another problem with taking calcium supplements is that if the calcium is not needed, or if either the thryoid or parathyroid is not functioning—both of which have responsibilities for calcium metabolism—the body must get rid of it. The blood will be filtered by the kidneys to remove the excess, but this is when a person risks getting gravel or stones in the kidneys and bladder if the urine becomes too loaded with calcium. Therefore, a person can be toxic with nonfunctional calcium, but still be low in functional calcium.

Hypocalcemia can be complicated by a lack of functional magnesium. If magnesium supplements are taken but not properly metabolized, a person risks getting magnesium deposits in the kidneys and bladder. Apple cider vinegar will not dissolve magnesium deposits, but birch bark tea and birch leaf tea will. Boil one teaspoon of birch bark or birch leaf in a quart of water, and drink three to four cups daily.

People who have arthritis, but who want to take the liver and gallbladder flushes, can replace the lemon juice with apple cider vinegar. Or they can take cod liver oil and reduce or eliminate other citric acid consumption; then these flushes can be safely taken using lemon juice.

Another interesting aspect of arthritis is that in some cases it is treated with intravenous injections of gold. Molecular gold is injected, but it would be much easier on the body if gold were administered in its ionic form. It is fascinating to observe the results of these injections. Gold, as an element, is electrically neutral. A neutral has the capacity to stabilize the glands by acting as either an alkaline element, with a positive charge, or an acid element, with a negative charge. In this case the thymus gland uses gold as an activator. Among the necessary nutrients of the thymus is silicon, which gives elasticity to tissues and strength to bones. Silicon accumulates solar energy, of which gold is a physical form. Gold has sunlike properties. Silicon enables the gold to be better utilized by the thymus.

The thymus is the regulator of the immune system, and it depends upon a person's total health and consciousness to create resistance. As a person's immune system becomes more functional, he becomes more radiant, more sunlike. He becomes unconditional in involvement. He also begins to be less judgmental and self-righteous, which are stagnations caused by holding onto opinions and beliefs. Therefore, the mind is not as rigid. As the mind starts to direct the body, the body becomes less rigid. The person begins to enjoy the freedom of listening to the opinions and ideas of others. He also employs his mental and physical flexibility by testing the validity of his belief systems. He can now put beliefs to the test, put them into action. He is further on his way to developing a knowing system. He is discovering life and his potentials through action, exploration, interchange, transformation, and letting go.

The essential aim of any therapy, including nutritional therapy, is to regulate energy. Sometimes that means speeding up energy; sometimes that means slowing down energy. Adding anything to the body which will make it lazy, that is, which permanently does an organ's job for it, creates difficulties. No artificial substance or transplant has the same level of activity or consciousness as the body does when that substance or transplant is put into the body. Either the body has to remake the substance or transplant to adapt it to its level, that is to its image; reject the substance or transplant; or adapt to the lower vibrations of the substance or transplant. If the body fails to do one of these three things, it will become poisoned by it. Drugs and hormones can help a person in extreme cases, as can operations, but therapies can always be used in conjunction with them to help the person understand why she has those symptoms. The aim should be to help the body reassert itself and help the person to stop interfering with the body's processes.

Let us return to the subject of the colon. A healthy colon is smooth and has good tone, which means that all the organs associated with digestion are functioning properly. The enzymes in the saliva are aiding with food breakdown. The stomach's processes for protein digestion are efficient. The liver and pancreas are secreting the appropriate amount and type of enzymes into the small intestines. The diet itself is providing the person with the necessary nutrients. Unfortunately, because of improper digestion and diet, and neglect of the liver and kidneys, a colon can turn into something which looks like a gas mask hose, complete with bumps and corrugations. In time, it can become a spastic colon, losing its flexibility. It goes into spasms, causing gas cramps. And food gets stuck in the bumps and corrugations, causing diverticulitis, an inflammation of the colon. Food ferments in the colon, rather than being passed. This fermenting food clogs the colon, and the gases disrupt the environment needed by the colon's bacteria to keep the colon healthy and operating properly.

The colon can go one step further on the road to deterioration. When it no longer has tone or elasticity and becomes inflamed, it is a matter of time before it becomes ulcerated. Those who have ulcerative colitis are often perfectionists who pursue perfectionism because they desire the approval of others. These are the perfectionists who would like to be sloppy or procrastinate, but do not dare to do anything in the way they would prefer. Consequently, because of a lack of true expression, their thyroids are depressed. They do not secrete the hormones necessary to stimulate carbohydrate, lipid, and calcium metabolism and protein synthesis. Without these hormones, digestion within their stomachs and intestines is impaired. They could get diarrhea because of nervousness, in which case they will have poor assimilation and possibly dehydration.

If the stomach does not have a good digestive capacity, it will not be able to act upon food, especially proteins. The gastric glands of the stomach need to be active to produce the acids which begin to break down the proteins into amino acids and separate proteins from carbohydrates. The colon is capable of working with carbohydrates, but not proteins. If whole proteins enter the colon, they begin to ferment and produce gas. The stomach needs to maintain a temperature of approximately 98.6 degrees in order to produce and secrete enough gastric juices, so cold drinks should not be taken with meals. And drinking during meals should be kept to a minimum, to avoid diluting the solid food's nutrients and washing away digestive enzymes.

A high percentage of people brought to hospitals with cardiac arrest first had indigestion and flatulence. They were not able to stomach it any longer, because of undigested, fermenting proteins. How could that be the cause of a heart attack? The abdominal area becomes filled with gases. Above the stomach is the diaphragm, and above that, in the chest cavity, are the lungs and heart; the latter needs space to maintain the appropriate rhythm. If a person gets upset or gets energy heat is activated. This whole abdominal area fills with gases, which are then heated. Balloons are sent into the air by heating gas, and that is what happens here. The gases expand and press the diaphragm upward. The diaphragm invades the chest cavity. The heart has to pump twice as hard to maintain its normal rhythm, and it also tries to push the diaphragm away. In many cases the pressure from the diaphragm alone causes the cardiac arrest. In other cases the heart simply cannot keep its accelerated pace for long. And being tense causes contraction of chest muscles, impairing proper heart rhythm. So, improper digestion can not only lead to the heart attack, but the stretching reduces the intestines' tone and hence the ability to move food through them. The possibility for another heart impairment is thereby increased.

Another Western malady which frequently accompanies flatulence and the holding back of emotional expression is lower back pain, or lumbago. Holding back emotional expression is another term for being nonassertive, and nonassertive behavior goes against one's own principles. Holding back expression can be caused by a fear of risk, a fear of losing something, or a fear of rejection. These unexpressed emotions can cause pressure in the intestinal area. Not only can that pressure go up and ultimately into the diaphragm, but it can also press against the nerves regulating the lumbar area of the spine, especially the hypogastric plexii.

The hypogastric plexii are two nerve centers. Each lies about three inches diagonally below the navel, one on each side of the navel. On women, these plexii are just inside the ovaries. These two nerve centers regulate the whole lower part of the body from the waist down. Every muscular action of the lower body is directed by these nerve centers, which branch off as specific nerves, including those that regulate intestinal muscles. When they tighten under pressure they do not give the neural commands, and the muscles lose their direction. The muscles over the lumbar vertebrae cross each other, and when digestion is improper, because the nerves of the plexii are tied in knots, they go into spasms and begin to pull. The result is that one vertebra goes one way and another goes the other way. If you are lucky a nerve does not get caught between the vertebrae, and all you have to contend with is lumbago. If you are unlucky and a nerve gets caught, you have not only lumbago but sciatica as well, because the shifted vertebrae put pressure on the sciatic nerve, sending spears of pain through your gluteous maximus and the backs of your thighs and legs.

You could adjust the vertebra to relieve the pressure on the nerves; but without relaxing the hypogastric plexii and alleviating the distress which caused them to tighten, the lumbago will soon be back. In other words, if you become upset enough that your digestive system is disrupted, you will get intestinal blockage and probably flatulence, which will also put pressure on the hypogastric plexii. This can become a painful situation if the pressure is never released, the plexii never loosened up, and the spine is never readjusted. The vertebrae will start to rub one another, and calcium spurs will form on the vertebrae. Movement will become increasingly painful as these deposits cut into tissues along the spine.

You can alleviate this condition in as little as five minutes with a self-massage. First, lie on your back on the floor, a table, a couch, or a bed. Put your feet down flat, so your knees are up. This will allow your abdomen to relax and become pliable. Now move each hand to a spot about three inches or so diagonally below the navel, one hand on each side of the navel. There you will find two hard spots, just inside the ovaries if you are a woman, which are knotted hypogastric plexii. Use your fingertips to rotate these two spots counterclockwise for three minutes and then clockwise for three minutes, massaging deeper and deeper until you get so deep you practically can feel your tailbone when your hands come together. After approximately six minutes of deep massage, the plexii relax, the muscles over the spine relax, and the vertebrae go back in place. If a nerve had been pinched by the vertebrae, it will slip in between them to its proper place, and the pain will be gone. In this case it is not necessary to do anything with the spine. You allow the body to adjust the vertebrae. From this relaxed state you can better work with what caused you to become tense in the first place.

Another common back ailment, which can be aggravated by working at a desk all day, is pain and burning between the shoulders. The first thoracic vertebra lies between the shoulder blades and is the site of the heart chakra. The inferior cervical ganglion is located anterior to this vertebra and supplies neural fibers to the heart and thymus. In many people that vertebra is twice the size of what it should be, and may affect adjacent vertebrae. That vertebra can be practically calcified in a person who is not expressing herself from the heart chakra. Her expression is still in the domain of the chemical state. She acts either from the root chakra, and does not transform her desire into unconditional expression, or her actions are predominantly from the spleen, and therefore spiteful and envious, or she expresses fearfully and angrily, never creating an environment in which the solar plexus can transform emotion and desire into transpersonal joy. Energy is stagnant, so the body is not radiant. On top of that, this person may feel obligated to carry the world on her shoulders. She worries and worries, questions and questions, thinks and thinks, and not only about her problems, but about everybody else's problems too. That affects her level of consciousness. She has less radiance and less resistance, which relates to the thymus, with the result that she picks up everyone else's problems. This is where the statement "God helps those who help themselves" comes in.

Carry your own cross. Do not give your cross to anybody else or take anybody else's cross. You cannot save anyone by trying to take his problems from him. Trying to do that is one of the causes of that back and shoulder pain. Then if you decide you do not want it anymore, you find it difficult to change, because your resistance is so low. No matter what is around, you pick it up. Your competence level goes down. Your lymphatic system becomes less active, because it has to use its energies to fight the invading mental toxins, as well as environmental toxins. Then the fulcrum between the higher and lower energies, the heart chakra, does not prepare the lower energies to be expressed by the thyroid. You have become a worrier instead of a warrior.

The word *worry* comes from the Celtic word *wyrgan*, which means "strangling, choking, suffocating." It is no accident that we say, "She choked!" if a person did not deliver or did not perform. A person who worries chokes herself. The thyroid and parathyroid are not merely hypoactive—they are being strangled! Those organs certainly cannot regulate metabolism while being choked! That is why it is not enough to simply give a thyroid extract, or magnesium, or iodine, or arsenic to activate this type of person. Too many other glands are involved, such as the adrenals, thymus, and pituitary, as well as a lack of understanding of the process of energy transformation. To get a lasting result, a person needs to realize she cannot assume anyone else's problems. She must also realize she has the responsibility to assert herself.

Do not let others cry on your shoulder. Do not have sympathy. Have empathy. Raise them to your level of energy. Your body forms a cross. It is the symbol for responsibility and transformation. It means there is only one person responsible for you: you!

For me to be effective and active in the world, I must be nonattached. Being nonattached is much different from being detached. The word *detached* implies no emotional involvement.

The word *nonattached* implies intense involvement, but it is involvement with no attention paid to the result. Being non-attached is like climbing a ladder. You attach yourself just long enough to a rung to pull yourself up a little higher. Then you have to let go of that rung, become nonattached to it as you trust yourself to find one higher, and proceed to the next experience.

In this life you need never worry about not getting affected by your environment. You do not need to look for trouble. There are all kinds of people and situations which will see to it that your path never gets covered with rose petals. But it is great that it happens that way. It gives you the opportunity to strengthen yourself, so you become a responsible person, that is, a person who is able to respond. You develop your potentials as you become more adventurous, more expressive. Then your thyroid functions better, your metabolism improves, your energy radiates. You become more attuned to the subtle energies which your body is capable of sensing and expressing. So as you walk down your road, you do not need to worry. If you encounter a road-block, simply move it aside—or go around it. Do not get upset. Do not question why it happened to you. Just know you have to do something about it.

You do not learn anything from knowing how to do something. You learn the most when you seemingly fail, by experiencing how *not* to do things. Learning this way is painful, but you have to have the courage and self-trust to go on. You have to avoid self-condemnation and saying, "Darn it, I did it wrong again!" Instead, say, "Wow! I did it wrong again! Now I know how *not* to do it, so therefore I am learning how to do it." It is learning in reverse. In time you will not need to fail as much, for there will not be as much to learn. But in the beginning, make an extra effort to be good to yourself. Know that you will learn and grow.

Recently I put my philosophy into action when we opened the Aletheia H.E.A.R.T. Center. We tried various methods of administration, programming, and communicating among staff. Our problems were growing pains. During this reorganization I had to say to the people, "Look, I have never directed a center before. I fall on my nose every day." But I immediately dealt with everything that tripped me, rather than falling and then waiting six months before I dealt with them. You can be sure that six months from now, I will still be falling on my nose—but for different reasons! And rather than sitting on the side of the road with my head in hands, moaning, "Every day I go to work, and every day I fall on my nose," I say, "What a marvelous opportunity! Every time I fall on my nose, I get the opportunity to be challenged to get up again and do something different."

Metabolizing Meat and Protein

There is considerable discussion these days about the role of meat in the diet and the pros and cons of eating foods derived from animals. Much misinformation is disseminated about how the body metabolizes food and the nutrients it needs in order to be fully functional. Today many food choices seem to be determined by fad or fear, rather than need. Neither fad nor fear is a good basis for food choices. As with everything else, diet should be determined by what you know and what you need as an individual. So let us take a look at how proteins are digested in the body and how eating meat affects the balance of certain amino acids and minerals, as well as how the body handles the byproducts of meat digesting.

Vegetarians claim you can get complete proteins from a vegetarian diet, as well as from a diet that includes milk, milk products, and eggs. That claim is true. A fact to consider is that nearly 98 percent of the ancestors of people who today live in Europe and the United States ate very little meat until about two or three generations ago. Most animal protein came from eggs, milk, and cheese, with a bit of meat being eaten only on weekends and festive occasions. Our genetic structure reflects this diet. Recently, as we supposedly have evolved, we have become more involved with Einstein's mC^2, which represents the denser forms and qualities of energy, as we pursue and identify more with material things. Consequently, we have started to activate our animal instincts, our primal feelings, more. That has created a greater need for animal foods, as we have entered and maintained this state of consciousness. We have become more carniverous, a change which reflects our resonance with a more material, or a more chemical, existence.

For most people a diet high in animal protein, especially meat, is detrimental to their health. This is fascinating, because meat is among the foods most complete in essential amino acids. But if protein is not completely digested, the result is toxicity. Eating some meat can be healthful, but if you have only a small war, why invite three armies? That is, if you have only a small need for that type of protein, why eat it daily, and by the pound? How much complete protein a person needs is determined by such things as age, health, size, and activity. The usual range is between thirty and forty grams a day, with pregnant and nursing women requiring about twice that amount.

Along with a heavy meat diet comes an excess of nitrogen. Nitrogen, which is part of certain amino acids and used in protein synthesis, binds with hydrogen to form ammonia, which is toxic to the body. Up to a point the kidneys are effective in eliminating ammonia from the blood. In addition, when more protein is eaten than the body can metabolize or excrete in a timely manner, there is an excessive amount of partially digested proteins, which consists of nitrogen and sulfur-based amino acids. These amino acids all want to work, but they are very selective as to what they will do. So there will be a high rate of unemployment in your body because these high-grade amino acids cannot be retrained to do other work. They are the maintenance workers, repairpeople, and builders of the body. You see, meat is not bad for you, but once the meat is broken down, what are you going to do with the leftover amino acids once your protein requirements have been fulfilled? So toxicity results from an accumulation of uric acids and nitrogen in the tissues and an excess of incompletely digested protein. These wastes can be eliminated by your waste treatment plant, the liver, and your filtration system, the kidneys. But with continual excess the body, especially the intestines, will become putrefied, not only by protein by-products, but all wastes associated with metabolism.

A heavy meat diet brings mineral imbalances to your system, mainly because meat has a tremendous excess of phosphorous in relation to calcium—twenty-two times more phosphorous than calcium. So here is phosphorous, which the nerves require, which emits light spontaneously, and which could give enlightenment— becoming detrimental! It becomes detrimental because, when an excessive amount of phosphorous combines with oxygen, rather than enlightening, it burns and can disrupt the nervous system. This is why older people are told to lower their phosphorous intake, but many times they are not getting enough sunlight or vitamin D to help assimilate their calcium. They have an excess of phosphorous in relationship to the amount of calcium they are able to metabolize. The phosphorous intake does not necessarily need to be reduced, but the calcium may need to be increased or made functional. Older people often take calcium carbonate, because it can prevent Alzheimer's disease. With it the brain gets more calcium and more carbon, with the calcium being an essential nutrient in its own right, necessary for neurological processes because it insulates the nerves and protects tissues from deterioration.

This counteracts the effects of too much phosphorous. Contrary to what some authorities believe, however, excesses of substances do not in themselves cause deficiencies of other substances. Substances need to be functional and to be in comparative balance with one another.

The interaction and exchange of substances between organs is what creates the body's electrical current and allows the energy of the body to be constantly in motion. If an organ does not produce or release enough substances, the body's biochemical and electrochemical environments will be disrupted. Either case causes toxicity and impedes not only the physical state, but the mental and emotional states as well. There are molecules which are not being activated, no appropriate transformation or exchange taking place. Organs interrelate and exchange energy through their exchange of substances. Energy comes forth during the building up and breaking down of different substances embodying different qualities of energy necessary to perform the body's myriad functions.

Ammonia, as an alkali by-product of the metabolization of meat, and uric acid disrupt the chemical environment of the digestive tract, and are especially detrimental to the structure and operation of the kidneys, liver, pancreas, and spleen. For example, ammonia breaks down the pancreas, which results in the spleen producing too few enzymes. That impedes digestion, especially in the small intestine. Consequently, food enters the colon which the colon does not have the capacity to break down. This food will hurt the structure and block the function of the colon. Some of the food, especially undigested proteins, will ferment rather than being digested. Diarrhea can follow, as the body attempts to turn this material into a liquid in order to get rid of it. Or there may be constipation if the body becomes dehydrated and the colon has become spastic, atonic, or ulcerated. This situation is complicated by the fact that the liver cannot produce all its enzymes when the by-products of excessive meat digestion affects its chemistry. It will not be as effective in producing digestive enzymes, converting and storing nutrients, synthesizing proteins for the blood plasma, producing the proper amounts of glucose, or converting toxins, such as ammonia, into less harmful substances which can then be excreted by the kidneys and sweat glands.

Because of interactions among the liver, gallbladder, kidneys, spleen, pancreas, and intestines, when any of these organs become less functional, the body's overall resistance to disease, especially to cancer, is reduced. Mental disorders are also more likely to occur. As the digestive tract becomes more clogged, the undigested proteins do not create enough peptides for the pituitary and other endocrine glands to produce their protein-based hormones. A heavy meat diet can also lead to premature aging and a lower life expectancy, because of chemical imbalances, a lack of assimilation of nutrients, and the build-up of deposits in the body's tissues. The deposits, waxy or starchy substances known as amyloids, are essentially the result of chemical imbalances. Amyloids are deposited within organs and connective tissues, weakening their structural integrity. They can especially cause problems to the heart.

Meat is hard to digest, because it is so dense. Digestion of it requires greater amounts of enzymes, time, and energy than all other types of foods. So if you are going to eat meat, be aware of what is necessary to metabolize it. Your stomach must be secreting the necessary enzymes and gastric juices to digest it. It needs the proper tone and temperature to do that. Liver, gallbladder, and kidney flushes will help keep your entire system clean, and thereby better nourish the pancreas so that it maintains its enzyme production. Your diet, of course, needs to include high amounts of fiber. Fiber prevents the digestive tract from becoming clogged, which aids in digestion, assimilation, and the movement of materials through it.

Let the person who needs to eat meat, eat meat. But the issue always comes back to each individual's physical, mental, and emotional state. A disciple once asked her guru, "Master, should I eat meat?" The guru replied, "If you can raise the meat to your vibrations of consciousness, there is no harm in eating meat. But as long as the meat can affect your consciousness, stay away from it."

There is an intelligence within this universe through which every particle can do exactly what it needs. Plants do not have the complex level of consciousness that humans do; they do not interfere with the process. They listen and follow the voice of Nature, the voice of the creative, universal force. Their consciousness is not higher or lower than ours; it is merely different. To some people the consciousness of plants may appear lower because they perceive plants as interacting with the environment in a very limited way.

But exhibiting a higher consciousness means allowing the creative force to flow unimpeded through the physical body in order to express individual potential to the fullest. And plants do that much better than most people! This is why I do not understand the morality of some vegetarians. They do not want to kill animals, because they can observe the consciousness and feelings of animals. But what do we know about plants? In their classic book *The Secret Life of Plants*, (New York: Harper & Row, 1984), Peter Tompkins and Christopher Bird discuss experiments that show that when you cut into a tomato which has audio testing equipment on it, a scream is registered. We do not know if it screams out of joy or it screams out of pain, but that tomato certainly tells itself it has been cut.

You need to take in foods which are alive in order to stay alive. You have the responsibility to maintain your health and maintain a high energy level so that your metabolic processes are efficient. Perhaps when you take in foods in such a way that your consciousness affects that of the substances you consume, you enable more particles to partake of new levels of consciousness, of energy, and of experience.

Though both plants and animals have a consciousness, eating meat can affect you more than eating vegetables. From an energy point of view, your level of consciousness and awareness has more in common with the direction and character of animals than it has with plants. Because plants take nourishment directly from the sun, soil, and the rest of the environment in forms more subtle than animals do (and consequently their consciousness is more subtle), it is easier for your body to break them down and remake them to your image. Animals and people do not take in as much nourishment in these subtle forms as do plants; people and animals are denser. Therefore it takes the human body longer to digest animal substances. It is more difficult to adapt them to the human form and vibrational state. If your resistance level is low and you are passion- or pleasure-oriented rather than joy- and happiness-oriented, you should limit your meat consumption. Those who are passion-oriented, chemical-oriented, material-oriented, and directed by immediate gratification, crave meat and other dense foods; these foods, in turn, feed those tendencies.

The interesting thing about meat is that if you raise your state of consciousness, you will not eat much of it. Another fascinating fact is that diseases associated with a diet high in meat are the same diseases psychosomatically related to people who are perfectionists for the sake of approval. They are the ones with spare tires around the belly. They are the ones who get ulcers, heart disease, and digestive problems. Of course, their proteins do not fully digest; they lay in the colon, ferment, and produce a lot of hot gas. These people are indeed full of hot air!

Meat can cause hyperglycemia because digesting it impairs the proper use of the element chromium. Chromium stimulates production of fatty acids, and is used by the pancreas as the active ingredient of the glucose tolerance factor, which affects the production of insulin. Chromium also aids in synthesizing cholesterol, that is, in preventing cholesterol from loitering in the arteries, especially in the aorta.

Metaphorically, cholesterol can be thought of as bricks. If you keep producing bricks and more bricks, but you do not have a mason to build a wall with them, you are going to have to stack them someplace. Because the mason, which is the chromium, has not come to use the bricks, the body stacks these bricks along the walls of the arteries. Chromium, as the synthesizer, keeps the processes which involved cholesterol going. The brain and other parts of the body have tremendous needs for cholesterol. To meet them, there needs to be an appropriate amount of chromium to direct the cholesterol to become involved.

Problems with cholesterol buildup can be related to the fact that most Americans are deficient in three elements: zinc, copper, and chromium. Because red meat has more cholesterol than it has chromium to synthesize it, the consumption of red meat is seen as a cause of arteriosclerosis. But without sufficient chromium, even if a person does not eat meat, he will have blocked arteries. And, ironically, blocked arteries lead to a deficiency of functional cholesterol. Incidentally, brewer's yeast is an excellent source of chromium.

Of course, a lot of American cattle are given steroids so the animals will eat more, gain weight faster, and so be slaughtered sooner. And because of steroids, many feedlot animals are concerned only with eating—so is it any wonder that people overeat? People are affected by the level of energy which created the meat they eat, so they themselves become preoccupied with food. Steroids also preserve meat. These add to the difficulty of digesting meat, and the liver and kidneys must work to eliminate them from the body.

It has been suggested that, in addition to meat, almonds, sesame seeds, soybeans, buckwheat, peanuts, sunflower seeds, pumpkin seeds, potatoes, and leafy green vegetables contain complete proteins. I cannot totally agree with that, because the nutritional quality of these foods depends on 1) the quality and type of seed which produces the plant, 2) the quality and ingredients of the soil available to the plant, 3) the care of and environment in which the plant is grown, and 4) the preparation of the food. But of the foods listed, I can say that, without a doubt, almonds contain all ten essential amino acids.

Essential amino acids are those amino acids necessary for building complete proteins which cannot be synthesized by the human body from other molecules present. The twelve nonessential amino acids can be synthesized by the body. When all twenty-two amino acids are present in the body in the proper quantities, complete protein synthesis can occur. Sesame seeds have all the essential amino acids, but not in the quantities necessary to be converted into a complete protein. All the other seeds usually have most of the amino acids, depending upon where and how they have been grown. In combination, grains, seeds, beans, and nuts are potent health-building foods.

When choosing foods it is preferable to eat those grown in your area, for you and they have both become acclimated to local energies. Thus is its easier for you to activate the foods' potentials. As long as you are influenced by your genetic structure, it is also wise to choose foods eaten by your ancestors. Once you become radiant you will have transcended your genetic structure and thus made it your own. You will be free from that past. DNA and RNA are very much involved in the evolutionary processes of your body and will evolve if, through a more involved state of consciousness, there is a freer flow of energy, that is, awareness and expression. Consciousness is a state of energy which is capable of activating energy. The more energy is activated, the more it expands. That increases its amplitude, as well as allows it to interact with more and more subtle energies. In other words, consciousness expands when all substances in your body are functional and transformational. You cannot expand consciousness without expanding energy.

Vegetarianism and Food Combinations

Those vegetarians who eat eggs, milk, cheese, yogurt, kefir, and the like will have a much easier time getting the essential amino acids which are necessary to synthesize complete proteins than do strict vegetarians, that is, those who ingest no animal products at all. Incidentally, fermented foods, such as yogurt and cheese, are necessary to maintain the intestinal bacteria needed in order to digest food and keep the intestines functioning. Strict vegetarians need to study their diet a little more and learn to combine their foods properly to ensure they are able to synthesize the necessary amount of complete protein. A vegetarian diet which lacks the proper amount of amino acids is just as detrimental to good health as complete, but not properly digested, proteins. Proteins are essential in building and repairing the body. They are also the prime component of most hormones, such as insulin and adrenaline, as well as enzymes.

Most of us need to consume vegetables of different colors. Many vegetarians and dieters think that a green salad is the healthiest food on Earth. But many green vegetables (remember that green is a cool, life-preserving color) will not sufficiently activate either physical or mental qualities. That is why people who follow an improper vegetarian diet look dull, feel dull, and lack energy.

What is necessary in the diet are vegetables which have red in them, a physically activating color, and vegetables which have yellow or gold in them, colors which are warm and which represent sunlight and can activate consciousness and mental potentials. Vegetables of orange or purple also have a high degree of activating energy awaiting release. White vegetables, such as some potatoes and the inside of radishes, contain all colors, of course, meaning they have a variety of vitamins, minerals, and various kinds of carbohydrates. Salads, soups, plates of raw vegetables, and mixtures of slightly steamed vegetables ideally will contain about seventy percent nongreen vegetables to thirty percent green vegetables. When such dishes are topped with sauces, sprouts (which can be left in the sun a day or so before eating them to increase their chlorophyll content), cheeses, or nuts you will have exciting and colorful meals. It is best to eat raw vegetables at room temperature, to avoid cooling the stomach.

For variety and nutritional balance, you can eat different colored fruits too. Vary your intake among fruits which contain different amounts of acids and sugars. Acid fruits include grapefuits, blackberries, citrus fruits, pineapples, strawberries, and raspberries. Subacid fruits include apples, blueberries, cherries, grapes, kiwis, papayas, peaches, and pears. Sweet fruits include bananas, grapes, and most dried fruits, as drying increases their relative sugar content. Melons are in a separate category and include cantaloupes, casabas, crenshaws, honeydew melons, and watermelons.

When you combine foods properly, you eat them in a manner which assures efficient digestion. For example, enzymes which digest proteins are different from those which digest carbohydrates. When released in the gastrointestinal tract at the same time, these enzymes have a tendency to inhibit one another's processes, so the body needs more energy in order to produce more enzymes. Whereas foods high in protein, fat, or starchy carbohydrates impede digestive processes when eaten together, each of these food types combines well with nonstarchy carbohydrates, which are green vegetables. Starchy carbohydrates include most roots, tubers, grains, legumes, and nongreen vegetables.

Fruits, though technically considered carbohydrates because of their high sugar content, are so different from the starchy and nonstarchy carbohydrates that they can be considered as a food group unto themselves. They contain simple sugars, which are the easiest and quickest foods for the body to metabolize. Because of their cleansing effect on the digestive system, it is best to eat them without combining them with other food groups, although fruits eaten within the different fruit groups may be eaten together. Melons, however, are best assimilated when eaten with no other food.

Every diet should contain an adequate quantity and quality of proteins, carbohydrates, and fats. What is adequate? That depends upon each individual, but a general guideline is 421 CPL. That means a diet which consists of four portions of carbohydrates, two portions of proteins, and one portion of lipids, or fats. Remember that carbohydrates include starchy and nonstarchy foods, as well as fruits. This formula should include a variety of foods, and can be adapted to whatever your needs are. Once your system and activities are in relative balance, you may find that the 421 CPL diet will help maintain a streamlined body.

In addition to the pleasures and social interaction associated with dining, the purpose of eating is to activate energy from nutrients which you have been unable to attract directly from the environment. Dietary needs are a product of each person's state of consciousness, and what a person eats will affect her state of consciousness to an extent which depends upon the total health of that person.

Nutrition, therefore, is an important aspect of expression for the body; it is the means by which you become conscious of your individual mind and soul. That is why most religions have rules about diet; food affects your spiritual state of being. When you attempt to follow or embody a holistic concept or a spiritual concept, you are attempting to harmonize your being: body, mind, and soul. And, as nutrients work with the body and as spiritual essence is included in the body, if you do not have a properly functioning body, you cannot have a total spiritual experience. Some dilution and adulteration of energy is occurring.

Many people hold their noses in the air because they think that they are more spiritual than others—holier than thou. But when you see how they live, you discover that they are great with words but take little action. They do not understand what needs to be done in order to maintain their whole beingness. Mentally they have become stagnant; they are not involved and are not developing knowing systems. That is when the digestive organs and the waste-eliminating processes of their bodies begin to shut down. Sewage gets backed up and the generative processes become less active. Why? No—or very conditional—action! They seem to feel if they have no intercourse with life, they become more spiritual. But they cannot be reborn with no regeneration or involvement occurring; that is possible only if nutrients are activated to bring their bodies to a transformational state of enlightenment.

Throughout this book I have described how the body operates on physical and biochemical levels, as well as being an instrument of transforming energy from light to fire to light. This is a critical point in the understanding of the processes of health and energy transformation. Perhaps no other element demonstrates this so well as phosphorus. Phosphorus is not very active unless another element is added to it—oxygen. With oxygen and phosphorous come combustion, or enlightenment. For this reason phosphorous is found in the body in the form of phosphates, a combination of hydrogen, phosphorous, and oxygen. When combined with oxygen, phosphorous becomes extremely powerful; it becomes phosphorescent in the body. Next to oxygen, it is probably the most powerful element associated with the body's metabolism.

The body's two highest energy centers, the pineal and the pituitary, channel high-energy information. And because all information comes initially as light to the body, both glands need phosphorous, a light-transmitting substance.

The thyroid, the next lower energy center after the pituitary, does not require phosphorous, as it is concerned with expression rather than enlightenment. But the thymus, which is regulated by the heart chakra through nerve fibers, needs phosphorous. Phosphorous helps the thymus metabolize nutrients and also is a synthesizer for substances produced by the thymus, entering in processes which transform and transmit various biochemical and electrochemical energies.

A gland does not operate only by nutrients. It also has "workers" for these nutrients, which enable the nutrients to be functional. These workers are elements which resonate with the base color and energy of the energy center, or chakra, which regulates a gland. Phosphorous resonates with the frequency and amplitude of the energy emitted by the heart chakra, which can be seen as the color gold. Phosphorous and other elements, such as silver and magnesium, share a relationship with the amplitude and frequency of the energy of gold. They are drawn in by the heart chakra and become part of the working environment of the thymus. These substances exist as electropotentials outside the body, and become ionic and molecular within the body, where they enter into physiological processes of energy transformation. Remember that chemically the heart chakra is where the fire from the lower energy centers becomes light. Any situation where there is a need to enlighten or to elucidate, there is a need for phosphorous. Phosphorous is found in the pineal, pituitary, and thymus, because these three centers are all primarily concerned with consciousness and enlightenment, by which the rest of the body is directed.

In addition to listing the nutrients required by each organ, Appendix B of *Human Energy Systems* shows the elements which resonate with the base color associated with the chakra that regulates the activities of each organ. Every particle in the body interacts with every other to some degree, and when organs share a need for certain nutrients or similar elements, those organs participate in transformational processes together. These processes can be observed as hormones, enzymes, or molecules which are produced by one organ and used by others to fulfill their physiological functions.

For example, let us look briefly at a situation where a lack of functional phosphorous causes miscommunication between the pituitary and the adrenal. The pineal and pituitary need a high degree of conscious direction in order to be fully functional. The pituitary is responsible for putting the satellite news of the pineal into action in the body, which is why it secretes so many hormones. The pituitary is subject to malfunctions which affect other parts of the brain as well as organs to which it has a direct hormonal link. A person with a malfunctioning pituitary can become indecisive or begin flitting from one thing to another without following through. In more extreme cases the person may become schizophrenic or exhibit manic-depressive characteristics from time to time as the chemistry of the body changes.

Many people diagnosed as manic-depressive are given hormones to activate the adrenal gland. It is not realized that the adrenal gland, especially the adrenal medulla, begins to malfunction because the pituitary is unable to properly synthesize the energies stimulated by the emotions. In other words, therapy can be directed at stabilizing the pituitary as well. How do we know there is a direct link between the pituitary and the adrenal gland? Because these organs share a need for four nutrients: iodine, manganese, phosphorous, and sulfur. The emotions stimulate the limbic portion of the brain which regulates various aspects of behavior. Impulses go from the limbic system to the hypothalamus, which then affects the pituitary by telling it directions, or asking it for directions. In a manic-depressive person the pituitary cannot function properly, because it is deficient in functional phosphorous. It does not have the light. It may be misinterpreting the information. It may not be responding to it at all. In any case, without phosphorous the pituitary cannot help bring the emotional state up to a more enlightened level upon which the mind and body can act and prepare it for transformation in the thymus so it can be expressed. Without functional phosphorous active in the pituitary, the anterior pituitary begins to excrete too much adrenocorticotropic hormone (ACTH). Because the amount of ACTH is excessive, the adrenal does not receive appropriate hormonal direction from the pituitary, and so the person becomes manic-depressive.

The adrenal cortex is supposed to be activated by ACTH, but when ACTH is present in excess, it is in a constant cycle of first increasing, then decreasing, production and secretion of hormones of the adrenal cortex. When that happens the person cannot work through his emotional states evenly, and so goes into a manic-depressive state. To overcome this situation the pituitary must be activated, so that it may see the light. It needs to synthesize the information coming from both the pineal and the rest of the body in order to elucidate upon that person's function, so that person knows what his function is and has a body capable of expressing it. Those are keys to maintaining an excited, radiant state.

People who are spiritually oriented may do all kinds of spiritual exercises in order to understand spirituality, but may be preoccupied mostly with the philosophy of spirituality. Trying to embody spirituality affects the emotions. Those who have not yet adapted their bodies to express that state of consciousness may feel stagnated and frustrated because of it, if indeed they realize the need to give their philosophical ideas form. If they merely want to have ideas with no form, they still will not have the activity necessary to get excited about their philosophy. In time they will become disenchanted with it. In either case the body is not adapted to emotional expression. These spiritual people can become manic-depressive because of it. This state will aggravate their situation if they try to hold onto a philosophy which tells them they have to be good and loving, never violent or angry. But they *are* violent and angry, and it is because the pituitary is excreting too much ACTH, which represses emotional transformation. When energy becomes blocked at the adrenal, or the solar plexus, if you will, in time that energy will tend to be expressed violently, whether it is directed inward or outward.

Research has been done on the amount of ACTH present in the body during different types of situations. One study first took a urine sample from approximately one hundred subjects to measure the amount of ACTH present in their bodies. Then the subjects watched a violent movie which included killing. The urine was tested again right after the movie, and it was discovered that there was a 60 to 70 percent increase in the ACTH, which would make the research subjects more prone to acting violently themselves. Later, urine was tested before and after the subjects watched a soothing documentary on plant life. The ACTH stayed relatively stable. This and other studies suggest that sensory perceptions, as well as subliminal input, can trigger drastic chemical changes in the body. Resistance to these stimuli can be increased with enough phosphorous in the body, particularly in the pineal and pituitary. The combined power and activity of phosphorous with oxygen means that more chemical energy is broken down into a finer state, which activates a more subtle energy that manifests itself as radiant energy—light.

In addition to being required by the pineal and pituitary, phosphorous exists (primarily as phosphates) in the various tissues and fluids of the body. Large amounts of phosphates are lost from the body daily, including about three grams from the urine and about one and one-half grams from the feces. So it is necessary to consume foods that contain sufficient organic phosphates to replace that amount, and tissue salts can aid in metabolizing these phosphates in the body.

The body needs five phosphates. Potassium phosphate is used by the brain and the nervous system, as well as the muscles and nerves. Calcium phosphate is essential for the sound formation of bones and teeth, and for proper growth. Sodium phosphate is needed for the regulation of the alkaline–acid balance in the body and to help decompose fatty tissues. Iron phosphate, as a major constituent of hemoglobin in red blood cells, controls the distribution of oxygen throughout the body via the blood. Magnesium phosphate is essential to the metabolic processes of the body's nerves and muscles.

No matter how intuitive you may be, without the phosphorous in your system being constantly replenished, you will continually be rethinking and rationalizing your situations, because the pineal and pituitary will not be able to elucidate the satellite news and put it into appropriate form throughout your body. A lack of phosphates might cause insomnia, because thinking may constantly be going on. Without functional phosphates, the mind and body will never be in harmony. As with every other nutrient, however, the phosphates must be present in levels at which they are optimally functional, and substances with which they interact must also be present.

The Thyroid

Because it regulates your rate of metabolism and regulates how efficiently you metabolize food, the thyroid figures prominently in how well you can express what you feel and what you are. A functional thyroid is vital to the appropriate expression of your potentials, of the I-self, of the id, and of the higher self, the entity. Appropriate expression, which requires a blend of these two aspects of consciousness, gives you your id-entity, your identity.

The thyroid is the gland responsible for the primary metabolism of substances the whole body needs, substances such as carbon, calcium, magnesium, and fluoride. Its hormones also affect protein synthesis and the breakdown of carbohydrates and lipids. The thyroid functions as a catalyst, capable of activating both catabolic and anabolic actions. Catabolism breaks down and activates dense, molecular substances, preparing them for assimilation, and anabolism reforms denser substances into more subtle forms of energy. As a catalyst the thyroid also activates both anions, negatively charged electropotentials, which break down substances, and cations, positively charged electropotentials, which form new substances and bring them into a more creative state. The catalyst, the thyroid, regulates the rate of these reactions.

If the body is sluggish, if there is a lack of appropriate expression, one which blends the facets of the id with the entity, or a lack of willpower, many times it is partly due to the fact that the catalytic action of the thyroid is weak. I have seen hypothyroidic people who have been given thyroid extract for years in order to regulate the metabolism. In some cases such treatments can be healthful, especially if the thyroid has been removed because of cancer or injury. But in other cases it makes little sense to do this if nothing else is done to activate the person's thyroid. For a person with a complete but malfunctioning thyroid, it needs to be determined why it has malfunctioned, and its appropriate rhythm and hormonal secretions must be reestablished. If the thyroid, for example, is doing some of its job, and the person is given a thyroid supplement to speed up metabolism, that person's metabolism may increase for a while, but the activity of her own thyroid will decrease. The medication will make her thyroid lazier. To enable the thyroid to regulate itself, the activity of the pituitary and the adrenal, as well as the person's way of life, attitudes, desires, and expressions of joy and willpower, must be considered. Whether the thyroid is hypoactive or hyperactive, it is because something has interfered with that person's appropriate and joyful expression and fulfillment.

I often suggest to people who have destabilized thyroids that they take arsenic albumin, a biotonic with the electropotential of pure arsenic. Arsenic is poisonous only in its molecular form. As an electropotential it is not poisonous. Its highly negative charge makes it very activating. It serves as a catalyst which energizes the thyroid and reestablishes its proper metabolism, creating the appropriate activity between catabolism and anabolism. Iodine is considered to be the element for the thyroid, and it is true the thyroid cannot function without it. But iodine is usually sufficiently present in the diet, though it may be in a compound form which is not active enough to stabilize the thyroid. Arsenic albumin taken with potassium iodine is a great combination for the thyroid. The arsenic will give the thyroid a boost, and the potassium iodine will activate the existing iodine, which is important, because iodine, in its nonfunctional state, is highly toxic. So until the thyroid is regulated, foods with iodine in them, such as sea salt, can be detrimental, adding to the toxicity of the thyroid rather than activating it.

A few years ago a product came out on the market, a combination of vitamin B6, lecithin, and kelp, which was supposed to be of tremendous benefit for some people. Six months later I was getting this product's victims in my counseling room, all of whom had underactive thyroids that had gotten worse with the use of this product. The problem was that the kelp, which is high in iodine, had stagnated the thyroid instead of activating it. Why? One reason is that kelp is green, and green is a life-preserving and energy-preserving color, but it is not an activating color. The kelp essentially was cooling down these people's thyroids, which was the last thing they needed. Kelp can be helpful for those with an overactive thyroid. But for those who have an underactive thyroid, reddish kelp, known as dulse, is helpful. Both dulse and kelp have a similar amount of iodine, but the composition and functions of the two are different. The red kelp activates and the green kelp preserves.

Botanical and herbal substances can be powerful indeed. Their goodness or badness depends not so much upon their qualities as upon your needs. Even if you know nothing of chemistry or the properties of plants, if you keep in mind the qualities associated with specific colors you will get a good idea of the qualities of the substances which are those colors.

Functions of Zinc and Copper

I mentioned earlier that many Americans are deficient in zinc, copper, and chromium. I discussed the fact that chromium synthesizes cholesterol, which helps keep the arteries free from blockage. The acceptance of the fact that people even need these metals is a relatively new development in traditional medicine. A few years ago a physician colleague laughed at me when I told him he was deficient in copper and zinc. He said zinc was good for gutters, and copper was great for plumbing and wiring. Today there are volumes of medical books with hundreds of pages documenting evidence and symptoms of zinc and copper deficiencies.

Why are many Americans deficient in functional zinc? Because many Americans drink alcohol. After you consume an ounce or two of alcohol, at least 50 percent of your body's functional zinc is eliminated from your body via urine. And it's also true that zinc may be in your body in molecular form, but enzymes are needed to break down those molecules. To complicate matters, many of these enzymes need zinc in order to be activated. This makes it difficult for your body to metabolize zinc. If you have a drink every day after work and you are under stress, in time it will be rare for you to have enough zinc functioning in your body, even if you eat foods containing zinc.

Zinc is a necessity for the health of male sex organs. Zinc activates the testes to produce sufficient testosterone, the male sex hormone. Because it is needed for testosterone production, a lack of zinc can keep a man from producing enough viable sperm. Some 58 percent of the zinc in the male body is used to maintain the proper functioning of the prostate gland. If a man has a longtime deficiency of zinc, it begins to show up between the ages of forty-five and fifty, especially in problems with the prostate. Many men who consume a great deal of alcohol no longer have the desire for sex, nor do they have much longevity in the sex act if they do want it. If they lack zinc, they probably also lack the copper necessary for sexual activity. They become afraid of sex, because they are afraid they may not be able to perform. They claim to be too tired. They may lose their erections halfway through the act. They may experience a lack of ejaculation or they may ejaculate prematurely. They may struggle for endurance, but in order to have endurance you have to have something with which to have endurance. I mean, if you have just a little water in a bucket, you can pour it out very, very slowly and thereby increase its endurance, but that is not going to increase the power of it. As a matter of fact, slowing it down weakens its power. Pacing oneself is not the answer. Energy needs to be activated, not saved!

The lack of power and desire generated in the gonads will reduce the total amount of activity occurring elsewhere in the body, because the arousal state, the masculine kinetic power, which is so necessary for joy and for having intercourse with life, is missing. If a man still has desire, but cannot use the energy generated by his desire, it means he cannot transform that energy through the other parts of his body. When activity of the generative organs declines, soon the adrenal gland may not function properly. Then all the other higher organs may be affected by the lessening of kinetic power.

Though not all of medical science agrees with me, my observations suggest that zinc is also necessary for the production of female hormones by the ovaries and for the functioning of the uterus. It is becoming accepted, however, that a lack of zinc impairs menstrual regulation, because the pineal gland, which also requires zinc, will not produce the appropriate regulatory hormones without it.

People deficient in zinc get sclerosis of the liver, because zinc is necessary to maintain the structure and function of that organ. Zinc may activate as many as one hundred enzymes, including twenty-five to thirty-eight enzymes in the intestinal area, thereby aiding in the metabolism of food and synthesis of other substances. These processes produce wastes which the liver is supposed to break down. If the liver cannot break down the waste products, the kidneys cannot filter them and the wastes will disrupt the rest of the body's chemistry. Zinc also helps the liver synthesize and store such vitamins as vitamin A. In addition, zinc enables the pancreas to produce insulin, a lack of which leads to diabetes.

After the zinc requirements of the liver and pancreas are satisfied, zinc is used in tissues throughout the body. Zinc is necessary for the fast and healthy regeneration of the skin and aids in general healing. A deficiency causes dry, itchy skin, and sub-cutaneous tissue loses its structure and tone, which causes wrinkles and premature aging of the skin. A person with this type of skin condition lacks silica as well as zinc.

Zinc also helps maintain the thymus, as it is necessary for the production of lymphocytes and antibodies. Your eyes use 14 percent of your zinc. If there is no zinc for the gonads, liver, and pancreas, which assimilate it first, there is no zinc for the eyes. This is the link between advanced diabetes and retinitus pigmentosis, a form of blindness. Your hippocampus uses 17 percent of your zinc. The hippocampus is the highest part of the brain stem. You could call it the Grand Central Station of all sense perceptions the limbic brain receives. The hippocampus is the neuron distribution center of those perceptions and directs them to other parts of the brain. When the hippocampus is desensitized, there is less acute sensory awareness, including a loss of the sense of touch. The hippocampus works with your emotions and memories, especially long-term memory. People without enough zinc, then, may become emotionally unstable and suffer from a loss of long-term memory.

The pineal uses 17 to 19 percent of your zinc. The pineal uses the zinc to aid in the production of melatonin, a hormone concerned with pigmentation. Many people who get prematurely gray or who have a receding hairline are deficient in either zinc or copper. Zinc is also necessary for the pineal to be able to produce the hormone serotonin. Serotonin is the neurotransmitter inhibitor and the metabolic activator of substances in the abdominal area.

Many people consume zinc in a chelated form. Their bodies may be strong enough to break down a pure molecular form of zinc, but a chelated form is usually a more concentrated form, meaning it is a denser molecule. In some forms 250 milligrams is concentrated into 50 milligrams. A chelator is then bound to it. The chelator grabs onto the zinc so the body absorbs it faster. But the chelator does nothing to increase the zinc's availability.

So the body has to work with a concentrated form of zinc, and also with the chelator. A common chelated zinc is zinc gluconate. The gluconate is an amino acid turned chelator, which is difficult to break down. So the body has to get the zinc back out of itself because it can do nothing with it. If you do buy chelated zinc products and your body has the capacity to metabolize molecular substances, try to find ones which have been chelated with amino acids other than gluconate.

Among its many properties, cayenne pepper is antialcoholic. If you want to reduce the amount of alcohol you consume, take a capsule of cayenne pepper two or three times a day. Soon you will have little or no desire to drink alcohol.

I am, however, certainly not saying, Don't drink. Some people, especially some older people, benefit from what doctors are now calling wine therapy. Wines and beer may have some chromium in them if they contain brewer's yeast and their alcohol content is not excessively high. Some older people may benefit from wine therapy because they don't get enough exercise, nor do they have enough blood sugar. For them, wine can be a type of tonic or body toner. It's great if they have a glass of port or sherry before bed.

The last of the three big metals in which most Americans are deficient is copper. What does copper do? In addition to being great for plumbing and wiring, copper 1) activates the iron in the hemoglobin of red blood cells so that it releases oxygen, 2) conducts heat and energy through the body, and 3) activates the liver to release glycogen. Therefore, in every case of hypoglycemia there is a copper deficiency.

People who cannot find what they are looking for or cannot remember what they are looking for may also suffer from a lack of copper. Though long-term memory is fine, short-term memory is poor, because the brain cannot operate properly without glucose and oxygen, and copper is involved in both processes. The short fibers of the synaptic nerve fibers, which are concerned with short-term memory, are affected first by a lack of copper.

If the situation is not corrected, in time, long-term memory will be reduced.

Because it conducts heat and energy, a copper deficiency can cause cold and chilling. It functions as your thermostat. When it is off you can either get cold, because your body cannot conduct heat, or you can get hot and get stuffy and feel you are not getting enough oxygen, which you are not. Copper serves as a longshoreman—it unloads oxygen from the iron, which transports oxygen throughout the body.

Because copper regulates the amounts of glycogen and oxygen available, people deficient in it need the heart to beat harder to get more blood, glycogen, and oxygen to the brain and rest of the body. They may experience palpitations and hyperventilation, show symptoms of amnesia, or get lightheaded and tire easily. Some people become nauseated when they eat, because not enough oxygen is available to metabolize their food. They sigh and yawn a lot in an attempt to get more oxygen.

Copper is also an antiarthritic because of its energy- and heat-conducting capacities, though not every person with arthritis is deficient in copper. A lack of zinc is likely to be found with arthritis. Bursitis is a symptom of not enough copper. Copper is crystallized sunlight, a lower grade of crystallized sunlight than gold.

Cayenne Pepper

Though it is always best to make changes in eating habits slowly and to detoxify the body first, a healthy body can adapt itself to and enjoy foods from different cultures. When we observe diverse cultures around the world as well as in our own country, we can see certain benefits as well as problems associated with their diets, ways of life, attitudes, therapies, and environments. Through our observations we can discover how they avoid maladies which plague us, especially diseases which our affluence causes, and adapt their ways to our needs.

Arteriosclerosis can occur in people who have mineral imbalances and who eat large quantities of animal foods, especially red meat. Red meat lacks sufficient quantities of two substances which could reduce the buildup of cholesterol in the arteries: chromium and lecithin. Whereas chromium synthesizes cholesterol, lecithin emulsifies it, that is, keeps cholesterol in suspension so it does not collect upon the walls of the arteries. Together, the two make a great team in battling arteriosclerosis. In addition, lecithin is also a vital nutrient for the nervous system and blood. Many of us live under pressure to perform, to produce, to get ahead, which complicates our mental and emotional stagnations. We need to keep both the nervous system vitalized and the blood flowing. Lecithin can help us do both. It is the source of choline and inositol. The highest-quality lecithin comes from the soybean.

In the Orient, where people get most of their protein from rice, miso, and tofu, there is a much lower rate of arteriosclerosis than in the Western countries. The reasons these people have very little heart disease and very few strokes, thrombosis, and phlebitis is first, they ingest mainly vegetable protein high in lecithin, and second, they have cayenne pepper with every meal.

Cayenne pepper has the capacity to break down hardened cholesterol and soaplike fatty substances. It can practically ream out such deposits from inner walls of the arteries, veins, and capillaries. Cayenne pepper, then, is a preventive for agina pectoris, spasms of chest pain usually caused by anemia of the heart. It also can prevent ulcers and arthritis, because it activates the circulatory system. Cayenne has a high vitamin A content, and its orange color tells you it has vitalizing energy; it is a life-promoting substance. Chili peppers, which are used by people in the Latin countries, belong to the *capsicum* genus, just as cayenne does. The color of these peppers ranges from a yellowish orange to fire engine red, with the orange ones being the most effective. The red cayenne pepper can be a slight demulcent and a slight irritant. Because you may get a burning feeling from it somewhere in your body, you may think it is bad to eat it. But the burning actually lets you know that something which needed to be activated is being activated. Cayenne does this because it has a high iron content (which its color tells you) and so is a very good blood oxygenizer. Cayenne pepper also acts as a blood pressure regulator. Blood pressure will probably go up if it is too low and it will probably go down if it is too high after cayenne is eaten.

I have seen many people who take high blood pressure pills. The pills are usually diuretics, which remove practically all the potassium from the body. A lack of potassium will disrupt the nervous system. Some people will become tired or depressed, others will become irritable. Medical doctors have become aware of this, so they also give their patients potassium; but if the patients have no assimilation capacity because of the drug, then the potassium they give them is not going to do any good. They are merely adding nonfunctional potassium to nonfunctional bodies.

It is virtually impossible to take too much cayenne pepper. In the liver flush, for example, a knifepoint of cayenne is recommended; that is a maintenance dose. Using it as a spice with your meals is also a maintenance dose. For a curative dose, such as for ulcers or high blood pressure, take at least one or two capsules daily. You can make the capsules yourself by filling empty gelatin capsules, available from most health food stores, with cayenne. The cayenne may burn an empty stomach initially, so you can buffer it by taking the capsules with your meals. Cayenne can help you stay awake and give you a performance boost because of its oxygenation properties. Some people make a habit of taking it before they go skiing or engage in other sports.

Used externally, cayenne pepper can bring oxygen and heat to any place on the body where there is stagnation. It can be sprinkled in socks and gloves to keep your extremities warm. It is also a marvelous healer for open sores. I have known people who have had ulcerative sores on their legs for years. What I have done to get such wounds to heal is to make a paste with cayenne pepper. I mix cayenne with vegetable oil and flour and lay it on the wound about a tenth of an inch thick, and then wrap the leg with muslin.

I once treated a man who had had open sores on his leg for four years. I asked him if he was willing to give me any kind of payment to close that wound in four days. He was apprehensive, but finally said, "Yeah, but I don't know what you want." I told him I wanted him to dance for me for an hour and a half. He said he thought that was rather strange and then added that he did not know how to dance. I said, "Don't worry about it. You will." I put the cayenne paste on the leg and wrapped it in muslin. I asked him to leave it on for four days and not to bathe it. He wondered when he should pay me. I said, "Any time now." In less than five minutes he started to dance, because the cayenne was burning his leg. He danced for an hour (he still owes me half an hour), and then the burning stopped. Four days later I came back, took off the muslin, and the wound had closed. As far as I know, it has never opened again.

Cayenne, then, is another substance which can be quite effective in distributing energies and a substance with which you can safely experiment. If you use it in a bandage for external sores, you should have a noticeable improvement in three to four days. If after four days the wound has not yet completely healed, prepare another muslin bandage and put it on the wound. In most cases another four days is sufficient time for healing to occur.

Exercise

For the past twenty-five years, America has been rather compulsive about exercise. Exercise can be beneficial, and most people should engage in quite a bit of mental and physical activity, but I don't believe in following physical exercise fads. You need to understand what your motivation for exercising is and whether a particular form of exercise is beneficial for your body.

During the early 1960s I had a heck of a time trying to unknot people who had gone into hatha yoga without preparing their bodies for it and without exploring what yoga could do for them. Yoga was a way for them to impress their families or next-door neighbors by showing that they could get into the lotus position and had become good yogis. I saw knees damaged, spines twisted out of shape, and muscles torn. Yoga can be a stimulating form of exercise if its role in helping with body regulation through proper breathing is understood. But initiates need to gently prepare the body to gradually assume yoga positions and never force the body into pain. Also, Western people need to understand that many are simply unable to assume some of the extreme positions, in which case they need to find a suitable substitute to help them accomplish the same thing.

Jogging is another sweet activity gone sour. It is still popular but is seldom done correctly. For example, jogging should never be done on asphalt or concrete. It is best done on soft, resilient soil. Otherwise runners risk wrecking the muscles and connective tissues of their legs, knees, hips, and thighs. If breathing is improper, it will impede the brain, and a high concentration of toxins will develop in the muscles.

Next, the motivation for jogging, in many cases, is to reach a certain number of miles per day and to push toward that goal out of competition and faddism. If jogging is a status symbol, the mental motivation is questionable, so the physiological results will not be very beneficial. Indeed, activity can become damaging if the will is used to force the body beyond its existing potential rather than to direct the body in a cooperative endeavor, which expands potential.

The first order of exercise is to prepare the body for it by developing proper tissue tone. Then exercise will help maintain that tone and enhance health and radiance. Too many start to exercise when their bodies are in pathetic shape. Exercising then will do the body more harm than good. This explains why so many people feel worse than when they started, and why they stop so soon. Not only do they really not want to do it in the first place, because they are embarrassed with their physical condition, compare themselves with others, or feel at odds with their bodies, but the activity will begin to break down and stir up some toxins in their bodies. The next step is to eliminate those toxins. If that is not done, the body will have to work with the extra burden of agitated toxins. Many people will prefer to quit exercising rather than come to terms with what the body is trying to tell them. It is screaming, "Detoxify me first!"

In addition to activating toxins, exercise will activate the body's stored sugars and fatty oils. So proper deep breathing is vitally important before exercise begins, in order to oxygenate the blood. Blood is your transport system. The oxygen it carries enables you to burn the glucose necessary to nourish the brain and muscles. Unless proper breathing is done before exercising, the body will get little benefit from it.

In extreme cases, such as with body builders, we can see what happens when a person exercises fanatically, but has not prepared the body for it. Through their activity, body builders stir up toxins from the breaking down of fatty tissues, fatty cells, and fatty acids. Also, most of their sugar and oxygen goes into building muscle. Body building can starve the brain for sugar and oxygen, and body builders can become "brawn, not brain." The brain is about one-fiftieth of most people's body weight, but it needs one-fifth of all the sugar and oxygen taken in by the body. If most of a person's sugar and oxygen goes into the muscles, the brain cannot maintain its proper chemistry. If a person trains intensively for several hours a day, as serious body builders do, very soon the brain will become sluggish. Radiance drops, and emotions, sensory perceptions, and judgment are affected. This certainly is not the purpose of exercise, but it can become a result.

The body can operate with an oxygen debt. For a while it can release energy through chemical reactions which do not require oxygen, but later extra oxygen will be needed to eliminate the carbon dioxide buildup in the muscles and blood. Also, the spleen has an energy reserve, and will release extra blood into the system when there is an oxygen and energy debt. So some exercise with an oxygen debt is not harmful, but problems can occur when the oxygen debt lasts for several hours for several days a week.

During rest most adults inhale about four and one-half liters of air per minute. During exercise they may use as much as fifteen liters per minute, which makes for an air debt of more than one hundred liters in just ten minutes of exercise. But you can avoid creating this extreme oxygen debt through proper breathing before, during, and after exercise. Proper breathing keeps the body relaxed and increases strength and endurance, thereby improving performance through a more integrated mind–body effort.

This breathing consists first of breathing to establish the alpha state, or body regulation state. Inhale for a count of eight, hold the breath for a count of eight, exhale for a count of eight, then hold the breath for a count of four. After counting for several rounds to establish a rhythm, continue this pattern without counting. The alpha state may take several minutes for you to attain, but once you become familiar with how it feels and train the mind and body to relax, the mind and body will go into alpha almost as soon as you begin this rhythm. Alpha breathing combined with autogenics to induce a relaxed state can prepare the body for effortless, fulfilling exercise and performances. Once self-regulation is attained you can develop the theta rhythm breathing pattern, which will greatly reduce your oxygen debt during exercise. Also known as paradoxical breathing, because it is contrary to normal abdominal alpha breathing, the theta breath is accomplished by a powerful drawing in of the abdomen. This allows the diaphragm, below the lungs, to completely expand, and thus you get the greatest amount of air intake and energy from each breath. Because the lungs fill from top to bottom, rather than from bottom to top, this type of breathing fills the lungs more than any other and provides the body with the greatest amount of oxygenation per inhalation. When you exhale, the abdomen is pushed out slowly for a long exhalation.

Begin theta breathing by sitting erect. Then draw in the abdomen as you inhale for a count of four. Hold your breath for a count of eight, exhale for a count of eight, then hold for a count of four.

Then inhale: 1, 2, 3, 4

Hold: 1, 2, 3, 4, 5, 6, 7, 8

Exhale: 1, 2, 3, 4, 5, 6, 7, 8, 9, 10, 11, 12, 13, 14, 15, 16

Hold: 1, 2, 3, 4

Follow this pattern, increasing your exhalation to thirty-two, and then to sixty-four. When you can voluntarily control your breathing to get a relaxed exhalation for at least a count of thirty-two, your breathing will cause your brain to enter the theta state. So first your body becomes regulated through the alpha state and then you become able to act upon your spontaneous desires through the theta states. Awareness of your desires can be enhanced through exercise perceptualizations. More and more athletes are using this type of regulation. Once the body is relaxed and the neuromuscular pathways have been established for a specific sports performance, using a combination of physical training and mental perceptualizations, conscious attainment and regulation of the alpha state allows the athlete to begin the performance in a state of relaxed competence. The theta state allows for a certain amount of nonattachment, so the body performs under the direction of the mind without the anxieties associated with concern for the result. Nor is the athlete burdened with the oxygen debt associated with anxieties, which promote shallow breathing, or with a body not properly oxygenated before beginning exercise.

If you train yourself to exercise while maintaining the rhythmic alpha breathing pattern, then later, exercising in the theta state, you will not produce such a high oxygen debt. Also, it has been reported by runners that when they breathe with short inhalations and long exhalations while running, they do not lose energy, because they are in rhythm or harmony with the environment. They can even meditate while they run. When they finish their run they are not tired. They are not out of breath. As a matter of fact, they are more radiant. Running or any type of exercising done in this manner can be very healthful.

The first thing people who wish to exercise need to be concerned with is developing muscle tone. If electropotentials are not active and the nervous sytem is, in a manner of speaking, leaking potassium, it will not be properly stimulated. They might have all the glucose and oxygen necessary for muscle development, but without electrochemical direction from the nerves, they will still have muscle flabbiness. They need properly functioning biochemical organisms for muscle development. What causes the metabolic imbalance? Simply put, people are not expressing, so naturally there is a lack of stimulation in their bodies because they lack stimulation in their lives. They are worriers. They worry about getting tone. They could get it if they quit worrying about it, because then they would have a proper metabolism. Then calcium would function in the myelin sheath of nerve cells, so potassium, which is found in the nerves as potassium phosphate and which is one of the body's most radioactive substances, would not drift out. Potassium has a high energy level, but when it is just drifting nonfunctionally through the body it does not stimulate the tissues to get radiant. People need output. They need their phosphorous, calcium, magnesium, potassium, and sodium to be functioning properly in order to get what could be called vulcanization of the muscles, a process which imbues substances with elasticity and tone. Muscles get weaker instead, because if muscles are stretched when they are not resilient and, metaphorically, responsible, they lose what little tone they have.

In addition to developing muscle tone, people need to prepare themselves mentally and emotionally to accept the activity which they are about to perform. It is the only way to "become it," whereby performance becomes effortless and beneficial. The mind, through the brain, gives messages to the muscles through the nervous system. People need to feed the nervous system, and then feed the muscle tissue, so they become nicely vulcanized and "rethreaded" before they hit the track, the weight room, the tennis court. Tone is created by a state of beingness. People may not be kinetically strong, but when doing aerobics or any other kind of exercise, they have radiance and tone because they are mentally and emotionally in a good state. Then when they feel the need, they can quickly build the body, or adapt it to any function they desire. Through the mind and emotions they have created a metabolism which activates the nutrients necessary to build muscle tissue. Because they have prepared for the activity, they do not use sugar and oxygen to such an extent that the brain's supply is depleted. In other words, the oxygen and glucose are properly distributed. This excites muscle tissue and an exchange of electropotentials takes place. The more they radiate, the more their muscles show tone and radiance. So through activity and expression, exercise can be helpful; it is a necessity for most people in order to maintain health. Through exercise people can attain greater self-knowingness. Exercise can help activate sedate people, and help calm and regulate high strung people. In either case, the key is learning to channel the energies according to the desired effect. This conscious direction stimulates the nerves to direct the muscles to help people see desire expressed in the world, which creates greater excitement.

Chapter 6

Health, Wholeness, and Attainment

Since the 1960s there has been a change of consciousness in this country, as people assemble a more comprehensive picture of understanding and awareness.

During the past twenty-five years, many people have come here from other countries as teachers of methods to attaining consciousness, such as yoga and martial arts. Nothing in the universe happens without a purpose, and I have come to see the influx of these teachers as a confirmation that we are indeed going from the Piscean Age to the Aquarian Age. This represents an expansion of consciousness.

There are three stages of consciousness, which relate to the three stages of physical, mental, emotional, and spiritual beingness. The first stage of consciousness is health. Health is a natural, evolutionary, dynamic process of transformation. It is one in which we have not yet acknowledged that our minds and bodies are part of a greater whole and that we are, in our totality, transformers of energy. In this stage we see ourselves separate from that which gives us life.

The second stage is wholeness. This is the state of growing awareness I see today. It is a state where we start to follow the laws of health and energy regulation. We have become aware and are part of the dynamic process of transformation of the whole aspect of soul, mind, emotions, and body harmony, but we still have to pay attention to that wholeness in order to maintain it. We cannot say that the evolution to higher health and consciousness will happen no matter what. Yes, we have been given the potentials to have it happen no matter what, but we still must intentionally direct that consciousness. We can then achieve control of our personal lives and the environment, while maintaining harmony with the environment. As we evolve through involvement, we still have to follow the law of transformation and sublaws which relate to such items as health and nutrition.

The third is attainment, or holiness. We have gone from health, where we still have to pay attention to the law, to wholeness, and finally, to the last stage—holiness. We have become the Law. We no longer need to think about it. We can say we are experienced universal practitioners now, in whatever forms we occur. The forms may be on the Earth; they may be somewhere else. Holiness is not determined by a group of people who proclaim us to be sanctified. Essentially, we are all saintlike in the beginning! We remain so when we allow our progression through creative stages. Holiness is something we are already, but we have to be aware of it so we can become the law. Then we spontaneously follow the processes of the universe. That is Cosmic Consciousness. It is a point where one has total awareness or consciousness of whatever happens within the totality of everything.

A new culture is being built upon the mingling of all the nations, races, and denominations. This is a thrust toward a new worldwide consciousness, communication, and understanding. Light-based technology is one way the new form of instantaneous communication is represented. Light is the vehicle of all information. The more we embody the attainment of wholeness, the more nonresisting we are in our growth. Therefore, we understand universal changes and any form of transformation from light to fire and back to light. The healthier we become, the more radiant we become, and the more information we give back to the universe, contributing to the process of transformation. We are less resistant to transformation as we become the law of transformation itself.

The more radiant we become, the more spontaneous we become and the more power we have. The power is not kinetic power per se, but the power of information and communication; the power of relating. That is what relationships are based upon too. Any time we stagnate our health through a mental state we have to eat, because the mind is not active enough with the body to supply it with a light source to become fire. I think this is why we have used up so much of the Earth. We have not radiated! We have been taking but not giving. Our light should shine upon nature too, and allow us to get into harmony with it. We then nurture nature. Because society is changing and because known material resources are diminishing, every country is in a tremendous materialistic battle, the outcome of which we cannot foresee. Nor do we know if we will ever be able to materially pay back to the Earth what we have taken from it.

Fortunately, material repayment may not be the way to pay back our debt to the Earth. Consider that we might begin to pay back our debt by becoming individually more creative, creating a new society in which we produce more and consume less of the resources. The fact is, resources are always secondary. We have forgotten what the Source of the resource was. We need to go back to the Source, to the Source of light, which has the information, and create with that!

From an ancestral point of view, we may think, Oh, my God, my great-grandchildren! What kind of Earth are we leaving them? They are stuck with what we have done! Now I am not saying that we should have caused this or should not have caused that. I am saying that maybe our actions have brought us so far that we cannot pay back our debts in a material way. There must be some way to make up for that failure. To me, it means that at this time our material debts can be repaid only by awakening to the Source. We can start repaying through creativity, through intuitive knowingness, through visionary, futuristic ideas. We must give our ideas form and allow ourselves to go with change.

It is alarming that we have accumulated such resource and monetary debts in just a few years. We have to come to our senses, though the system is working itself out. Or I should say we are working ourselves out of the system. We need to be concerned about the direction of change and apply ourselves to change, but we do not need to worry about the health of the system itself. Light-based technology will help bring the information by which we can achieve a more universal, instantaneous knowing. We can use it to discover the answer to "What is my purpose? Wherein lies my power? Am I fulfilling my potentials?"

The individuality of each person is the strength and wealth of the universe. Each one of us contributes our heritage, potentials, and beingness. Until now we have been self-righteous and judgmental of one another's beingness. There has been much comparing and putting down of one another. World War II was a fight against the concept of a superior race. Millions were killed to stop the self-righteous people who would spit on us if we were not like them. But we have still been doing the same thing over and over, but in a more covert way, throughout the world. We have not granted each person fulfillment. We have beautiful phrases of freedom for this and freedom of that, but are we really tolerant of freedom? We allow freedom as long as people express their freedom in a way which the majority accepts. But we have a wonderful opportunity to change that now. In this New Age we can build a new heritage based upon knowingness and individual fulfillment.

Self-righteousness and judgment have occurred throughout the ages. What we have seen as harmony over the centuries has been more of a truce than a peace. As long as we fear change, we will be self-righteous. We will not appreciate the differences among people. Judgment is an analytical process. We judge because we do not want to change and adapt ourselves to new states. Why do we analyze and compare? Why does it strike me that you are different? Is it not because you are? We do not have to become and never will be able to become like anyone else, because we are all so unique. Why withdraw from one another because of fear? If we consider each person a facet of a jewel, we will have gone from self-righteous and judgment to freedom.

Perhaps you are a construction worker. Another person is a teacher. Why should this cause a difference in knowingness and self-worth? It does not matter what your experiences are. Whatever a person is, let it be. We must evolve from living solely by judgment and self-righteousness, processes by which things and people are broken down, and become a synergistic world in which each power adds to the greatness of the whole.

The universe operates in an orderly way, and because the universe contains all, we can say that the universe is the law. The universe does not follow the law, it *is* the law, so order is the law, with a myriad of sublaws representing different subdivisions of energy. It can be compared to a driver's license. When you get a driver's license, you agree to follow the law. In its totality the law represents an orderly way of driving. Sublaws include such things as driving 55 miles per hour on the highway, being sober when you drive, and obeying traffic signals.

Physical, mental, and emotional states represent levels of energy. Imagine these levels to be jigsaw puzzles. These are whole pictures made up of many pieces. The correct combination of those pieces gives us the total picture, because it is the proper relationship of the parts with one another which creates the whole. Disconnected parts simply cannot create a whole picture, so the whole is more than the sum of its parts. The whole represents a higher quality of energy, because of its organization. The whole is what we work with in holistic health.

But because I am not yet capable of knowing the totality of the level upon which I exist, let alone all the levels with which I interact, I have to dissect the whole into its parts. In other words, I have to analyze it. I might want to understand the sublaw of vibrations, the sublaw of resonance, the sublaw of comparisons, the sublaw of nutrition. The only way I can get to know it is by pulling the total apart, analyzing what I need to know, then putting it all back together again, that is, by going from analysis to synthesis. This process is called experience. Let us not criticize others for being analytical. If we did not analyze, if we did not pull it apart, then we could not put it back together again. We would be standing upon the whole picture without understanding it.

While we are in a state in which we have not totally enhanced our health, we need to pay attention to such things as nutrition, the Earth environment, and our personal environments. For example, day people, who need negative ions and sunlight, benefit from having light green plants wherever they spend much time. Light green plants help people reach a mental state that is comparatively balanced between positive and negative. The more space and light available in the environment, the better most people will be able to function. For more information about the effects of light on our health, I suggest Dr. J. N. Ott's book, *Health and Light* (Devin Publishing, 1973).

People vary in their sensitivity to construction materials, food, and clothing. It is virtually impossible today to be in an environment which is totally natural or to feed or clothe yourself in a totally natural way. Take as much prevention as possible and do not purposely choose unnatural settings, processed foods, or synthetics, but if these things are there, and they are, immunize yourself by increasing your resistance. For instance, synthetic rugs insulate you from the electromagnetic radiation of the earth, but because of the weave and porosity, some of the radiation comes through. Concrete is also porous and radiation comes through it too.

When you wear shoes with synthetic or rubber soles, you are insulated from the earth. The nerve endings of the feet get crystallized, because there is no radiation coming through to them. In other words, you are not grounded. When you are not grounded, you may get a bioelectrical short circuit. Electromagnetic energy is not flowing properly through your body. To counter this, some people take foot baths of shavegrass, which is high in silica, and silica tissue salts to decrystallize the nerve endings. This is important because all the body's organs have nerve endings in the soles of the feet. Because we are living in the era of the sneaker, more and more people are having problems with their feet. Their bodies cry out for stimulation, yet they never kick their shoes off and walk barefoot on the soil, through the grass and the morning dew. You have to have contact with the Earth. Walking barefoot can be very therapeutic. In Europe people engage in what is called dew treading. They walk in the grass early in the morning, when the dew is charged with the sun's energy and has the highest electrical charge and concentration of minerals. Through contact with the feet, the dew helps alleviate crystallization and stimulates the soles and nerve endings, enhancing the flow of energy in the body.

Synthetic clothing will also interfere with your energy field to some extent. Though it is always preferable to wear cotton, silk, or wool clothing, certain products are difficult to acquire in natural fibers. The loose weave of some synthetics does, however, allow a significant energy exchange to take place.

Remember, everything you identify with will come to dominate you. You can tell yourself, "Do this and don't do that" and "Wear this and don't wear that," but by doing so you give more power to outward energies to affect you than to your capacity to affect them! Healthy people are not just the people who wear natural clothing, or never wear sneakers, or eat only the proper foods. Quite often, it is their mental state which keeps them healthy. Conversely, those who mentally, physically, or emotionally identify with diseases, substances, or situations are much more likely to be affected by them.

This identification is one factor which can influence a person's sensitivity to certain substances. How much are allergies really caused by substances? How much are they caused by fear of the substances and what we say they can do? I once counseled a woman who claimed to very allergic to flowers, specifically roses. She came into the counseling room, saw the roses I had on the table, and stood there coughing and sniffling, with her eyes watering. I asked her why she had these reactions, and she said she couldn't handle roses. Well, I had purposely put silk roses on the table, but they looked so real that she suggested to herself that they were roses. The message she gave herself was, "A rose is a rose is a rose."

Mental suggestion is not the cause of every allergy. There are substances your body might not be able to handle at a specific time, because your immune system, which is related to your level of consciousness, is malfunctioning. You can stop wearing, eating, or using these products to avoid being affected by them, but where will it stop? It is like I can either build a bridge over a river or walk a hundred miles around it, so I never encounter it. You have the potential within you to work with these situations. People diagnosed as being allergic to a substance may find a year later that they react to a score of other things as well. Many times this happens because they have become more guarded, more self-protective, more questioning of their capabilities, drawing the energy in and condensing it out of fear, rather than expanding it and radiating self-competence.

Sometimes people switch to natural foods in an effort to become more healthy or to avoid allergic reactions. They do not realize that natural foods are more antagonistic to toxins than toxins are to toxins. So these people get bigger body wars going, charging their immune systems even harder to work not only with the toxins, but the natural foods too. When they are tested again for allergies, they discover the foods which were fine before have become irritants to them. No wonder! They have made toxins out of them. These people need to physically detoxify by taking liver and kidney flushes, salt baths, and enemas. They also need to detoxify mentally as well, and eliminate fears of what will happen if they wear this, touch that, or eat this. People make themselves toxic. Some people even say with pride, "Oh, I can't have that. I am allergic to it." They practically wear buttons proclaiming it and focus their whole lives on petty avoidance rather than intense involvement. They fight things and see things as enemies, rather than trying to transform the things and themselves.

Do not give your body extra burdens by walking around with fears. Put your attention into directing good, healthy energy to yourself. Get the energy excited! Get yourself excited so the body can start working on itself without interference. Every time you identify with and fight a disease, you turn your immune system into an army to kill and throw out the enemy, rather than allowing it to care for the lovely garden that your body is. Health is not a static state. It is dynamic and evolutionary.

The entropic state is an intermediate state between breakdown and buildup. The old is broken, the new is created. In the process a chaotic state which we call disease may occur. We do not necessarily need to kill it or try to repress it. If we allow the body to work the situation out by getting busy and excited, we might find ourselves more successful and healthy. Disease we can handle. It merely tells us that changes are occurring or that we need to make changes.

It is when we are ill that we begin to really have problems. Why? Because ILL is an acronym meaning *I Lack Love*. To become ill means we have been repressed for too long and have sought approval for too long, rather than loving ourselves enough just to be.

The universe changes constantly but we fight to stay the same. We have problems because we refuse to change with the world around us. Our minds get attached to things we have done in the past or to things we have lost. Energy that would naturally move toward the future stagnates because we make a futile attempt to fix things where they were.

Many people have the mistaken belief that it takes a lot of energy to change. It does not. Energy continually and naturally changes. Our job is to live in rhythm with those changes. If we do not fear change, we stay spontaneous and excited. If we stay excited no pollution or disease will affect us, because we are radiating a higher energy field. Remember, it is impossible for a lower energy field to enter a higher energy field.

You know that thoughts are energy. By their very nature, defensive thoughts lower the momentum of the energy field around you. As that momentum is lowered, your energy becomes dense, and you pick up all sorts of influences, such as fear, depression, and anger. Therefore you cannot accuse anyone or anything of taking your energy or draining you. If you feel people drain you, it is because you were unable to communicate appropriately with the people in your environment, and you got tired walking around with energy that could barely move. You cause your own energy drain. Even things you regard as unpleasant can be transmuted into occasions of joy. You can always choose to focus on some positive aspect of the experience and create joy, where before there was only resistance and resentment. Joy is hidden in its apparent opposite. The art of life is to find joy even when conditions lead you to believe it cannot be found.

We miss a lot when we fear change. Too often we live in the past. We say we live in the now, but that does no good when our now is based in the past. It must be based in the future. We need to challenge ourselves to become aware of how quickly everything becomes obsolete. The past is only a fraction of a second away, as is the future. Imagine how stagnated we have become, imagine how much time we have lost, when we have lived in the past for ten or twenty years! The more past we allow to pass, the more future comes into being. We have to realize we cannot be what we were two seconds ago, because if we are, then we stood still and failed to go with the transformation. There is no time to just sit and think about what we could have done.

We have to risk and do! The challenge is to be absolutely non-attached to the past and be attached in fascination to the future, thereby becoming good visionaries. By throwing out our lights to the horizon ahead of us, we will get clearer pictures of what the future can be. We can move toward that future and live it now. But we cannot see without lights, so we had better send some lights out. These lights are the lights produced by our own radiance. This visionary quest is a tremendous challenge for humanity. And our visions cannot be achieved with debilitated bodies and minds. It is that simple.

Too often we live our lives as if we were fighting forest fires. The more we fight the fires, the more smoke in our eyes, and the less we see what we are doing. We need to intensify our fires and desires. If we hold back our fiery states, if we keep throwing water on them, they will only smoke and smolder, never generating the energy to become light. It is the transformation of this energy which allows us to achieve our desires.

We are quite smoked in at the moment. We cannot see what we are doing. It reminds me of Jesus' cry, "Father, forgive them, for they know not what they do." How can we know what we are doing if we are in the smoke all the time? We must use the path of action to burn the fire of excitement. When excitement fills us, light is given off from what we have created. It is our creativity which will heal our planet and ourselves. As resources become more unavailable, we will be forced and challenged to discover the Source. We could have done with much less of everything if we had used our resources properly. The universe is a beautiful, biodegradable recycling plant. Nothing is lost in the universe. Nothing is wasted. Nothing is destroyed without something else immediately being created from it.

We are in a period of great change. If the thought of upheaval causes you to be afraid, you really have no choice but to challenge your fear. If you are afraid, trust yourself to deal with change and take comfort in your abilities. Too often we stagnate when we equate fear with pain, for then the fear of change becomes an enemy. Change is painful because we fear it. We put our energy into controlling rather than changing.

You have more options than fight or flight. To fight or to flee something means you have not dealt with it. You have just wasted power. Embrace challenge without destroying what it is you fear. Give that which you fear the right to be as fearful of you as you are of it, and then you can find a common base for a relationship, and that is everything in life. Encounter your fears. If you are afraid of something, put it on your horizon. Perceive and experience yourself working with that fear. If fear is a vicious animal, perceive yourself approaching that animal. Talk to it kindly. Establish communication.

It is amazing the changes you can see when you communicate with that which you fear. You do not need to control fear. All you need to do is to communicate with it, but you have to put yourself at eye level with it. You cannot perceive yourself as higher up than what you are trying to understand. If you do you will add to its ferocity, because although it cannot think in the same manner as you, it is sensitive to what you feel.

Fear of disease does no good. Fear reduces your immunity. Do not make disease any stronger than it is by giving it power through your fear. Do not give it power by declaring it to be your enemy and constantly warning everybody against it. The moment you attach yourself to anything or identify with anything, you become dominated by it. You can infect yourself with a disease by your state of mind as easily as you can be infected by someone else. Do not attach yourself to anything of a lower nature, not to a thought, not to fear, not to disease, by declaring it to be an enemy. Declare everything to be your friend. Declare everything to be part of the process of change. Learn how the processes work. Through physical, mental, and emotional activity and self-fulfilling expression, you will contribute to the radiant health of the universe and continuously increase the quality of your health, joy, and beingness.

You are a unique expression of energy, with needs, desires, and potentials. The key to health is creative expression. Do not hold back your capacities; be spontaneous and joyous in everything you do. Do not compare yourself with others and worry about whether your capacities are higher or lower than theirs. Just do it for the sake of doing it. Do not hold energy back for fear someone will not like what you do. Just keep bringing the energy up and out. Trust yourself. Know yourself. Be yourself.

If someone says to you, "Don't be so emotional," it is her way of telling you to stagnate because she is stagnated. She is not burning bright enough and hot enough to express her manifestations.

I say, "Be emotional." Keep the energy in motion. The more energy you radiate, the greater things you attract. The only way to keep your energy in motion is to put fire underneath the molasses of your personality and to allow the increased energy to make you thinner, more transparent. In this way you eventually become lighter, and evaporate into a state of illumination, returning as light to the universal Source from which you originated.

References

Duffy, W. 1976. *Sugar Blues.* New York: Warner Books.

Glasser, R.J. 1976. *The Body Is the Hero.* New York: Random House.

Green, E., and A. Green. 1977. *Beyond Biofeedback.* New York: Delacorte Press.

New Games Foundation, A. Fluegelman, ed. No date. *The New Games Book.* New York: Doubleday.

Ott, J.N. 1973. *Health and Light.* Greenwich, CT: Devin.

Schwarz, J. 1977. *The Path of Action.* New York: E.P. Dutton.

———. 1978. *Voluntary Controls.* New York: E.P. Dutton.

———. 1980. *Human Energy Systems.* New York: E.P. Dutton.

Tompkins, P., and C. Bird. 1984. *The Secret Life of Plants.* New York: Harper & Row.

About the Author

Jack Schwarz, Founder and President of the Aletheia Psycho-Physical Foundation for the past fifty years has distinguished himself as an internationally-recognized leader in practicing and teaching voluntary controls and human energy systems. He has counseled, lectured, and assisted in consciousness research throughout the world, demonstrating his abilities in pain control, blood flow, healing, and the voluntary control of internal states through which he knows greater consciousness can be achieved. He has the ability to assist you to self-healing with words, making use of metaphors, anecdotes, and teaching tales.

Jack has been a subject, researcher, and consultant at major biomedical and life science research centers in the United States and abroad. His most noted work has been with Alyce and Dr. Elmer Green at the Menninger Foundation in Topeka, Kansas; with Dr. Kenneth Pelletier and Dr. Joe Kamiya at the Langley Porter Neuropsychiatric Institute of the University of California, San Francisco; and with Dr. Paul Grot at McMasters University in Hamilton, Ontario.

Jack Schwarz received his naturopathic training in Holland before coming to the United States in 1957. He instructed Swedish massage and hydrotherapy in Los Angeles from 1957 to 1967. For the past thirty years Aletheia has been Jack's vehicle for educating and training people throughout the world in his health philosophy. His work is combined with the constant study of physiology, psychology, and healing.

Other Books by Jack Schwarz:

The Path of Action

E.P. Dutton, Publishers, 1977

The "Path of Action" is not only a way of life, it is a practical guide. Jack Schwarz explores the origins of his "talents" and explains exactly how he achieved his state of enlightened well-being. Jack Schwarz teaches you, step-by-step, how to meditate. He explains what to do and what to expect. *The Path of Action* will inspire all who wish to follow their path to enlightenment.

Voluntary Controls

E.P. Dutton, Publishers, 1978

Exercises for creative meditation and for activating the potential of the chakras (energy centers of the body). This is a tool, a handbook that gives specific step-by-step instructions to help you develop the remarkable powers of mind and body demonstrated by Jack Schwarz. Creative meditation is the key to increasing your overall energy state until you are creatively inspired in all your thoughts, actions, and words. Activating the potential of the chakras will complete the revolution in your life.

Human Energy Systems

E.P. Dutton, Publishers, 1980

Human Energy Systems describes a way of good health, using the human energy fields (auric fields), including special eye exercises, the Tarot system, and a guide to medicinal herbs.

Aletheia Foundation—Since 1958

The Aletheia Foundation dedicates itself to increasing harmony, health and happiness in the world by bringing forth integrative changes in individuals. Our programs, supported through research, educate people in practical and effective methods for achieving optimal health through self-regulation and self-management.

It is our utmost desire to promote innovative health education by blending experiential, educational, and research results with existing lifestyles and modes of health education. We wish to network with other individuals, medical, educational, and research professionals within our community, the nation and the world for the betterment of humankind.

Our programs with Jack Schwarz:

PHT —The personal health training program educates people from all walks of life about how various forms of energy and self-regulation relate to their individual health and well-being. The following trainings are included: voluntary controls, human energies, autogenic feedback, nutrition, mind–body assessment, massage and biotonics.

INTERNSHIP PROGRAM —Specialized training emphasizing self-regulation and the human energies.

ACCELERATING CENTER WORKSHOPS —Workshops given on the human energy centers, diet and nutrition, human energy intensive, transcending into knowingness annual intensive, children's PHT, exploring the paraconscious, energy in motion with light, color and sound, and super-teaching. Plus many more workshops and conferences throughout the year.

P.P.R. —Psycho Physical Rehearsal Intensive gives the Jack Schwarz method in autogenic training of self-regulation and self-management through the use of biofeedback and human energies.

A.C.T. —Aletheia Corporate Training offers the environment in which members of a team can discover ways of working together and increase competency by suggesting attitude changes which will open doors to creative productivity.

For further information and tools for study on Jack Schwarz and Aletheia contact:

THE ALETHEIA FOUNDATION
1809 N. HIGHWAY 99
ASHLAND, OREGON 97520

(503) 488-0709

Other Celestial Arts books you may enjoy

Staying Healthy with Nutrition by Elson Haas, M.D.
The long-awaited examination of how what we eat determines our health
and well—being. Truly a complete reference work, it details every aspect of
nutrition from drinking water to medicinal foods to the latest biochemical
research. $24.95 paper, 1,200 pages

Staying Healthy with the Seasons by Elson Haas, M.D.
One of the most popular of the new health books, this is a blend of Eastern
and Western medicines, nutrition, herbology, exercise, and preventive
healthcare. $12.95, 252 pages

What the Buddha Never Taught
by Tim Ward
Tim Ward's engaging, often humorous account of his initiation into a
Buddhist monastery is, by turns, iconoclastic and inspiring, full of
anecdote, insight and parable. $14.95 paper, 256 pages

The Ecology Cookbook by Nan Hosmer Pipstem and Judi Ohr
This "Earth Mother's Advisory" shows how properly nourishing ourselves
can bring about peace of mind, spiritual awareness, planetary peace and
healing, and a better environment. Includes recipes, herbal medicine, and
ecological advise. $11.95, 252 pages

Choose to be Healthy by Susan Smith Jones, Ph.D.
The choices we make in life can greatly increase our health and happiness
— this book details how to analyze one's choices about food, exercise,
thought, work and play, and then use this information to create a better,
healthier life. $10.95, 252 pages

Wellness...Small Changes That You Can Use to Make a Big Difference
by John Travis, M.D. and Regina Ryan
Geared to busy people, or those who are not ready to radically change
their lifestyle, this book outlines fifty small changes anyone can make in
areas including nutrition, relaxation, work, and relationships. The suggestions can be taken together to form a coherent wellness program, or
done one at a time as is convenient. $5.95 paper, 80 pages
A TEN SPEED PRESS BOOK

Self Esteem
by Virginia Satir
A simple and succinct declaration of self-worth for the individual in
modern society who is looking for new hope, new possibilities, and new
positive feelings about themselves. $6.95 paper, 64 pages

How Shall I Live? by Richard Moss, M.D.
A medical doctor and alternative healthcare advocate discusses how to deal with a major health crisis, and how to transform the experience into an opportunity for greater aliveness. Covers issues such as fear, guilt helplessness, and despair and shows how to release and share your healing energies. $8.95 paper, 180 pages

Moosewood Cookbook (expanded edition) by Mollie Katzen
This top-to-bottom revision of our bestselling cookbook retains all the old favorites and adds twenty-five all-new recipes. All recipes are as delicious as ever, and the lowered amounts of high-fat dairy products and eggs now reflect today's lighter tastes. "One of the most attractive, least dogmatic meatless cookbooks printed...an engaging blend of hand-lettered care and solid food information." —The New York Post. $16.95 paper or $19.95 cloth, 256 pages. A TEN SPEED PRESS BOOK

Friendly Foods by Brother Ron Picarski
Gourmet vegan food—no meat, eggs, or dairy included—from a Franciscan friar and three-time Culinary Olympics medal winner. "When it comes to elegant, dairyless vegetarian cooking, *Friendly Foods* is one of the best books available."—John Robbins, author of *Diet for a New America*. $16.95 paper, 258 pages. A TEN SPEED PRESS BOOK

Healing Environments by Carol Venolia
This holistic approach to "indoor well-being" examines healing, awareness, and empowerment, and how they are affected by various aspects of our environment. Its principles can be applied to homes, workplaces, and healthcare centers to bring greater peace and harmony into our lives. $12.95 paper, 240 pages

Available from your local bookstore, or order direct from the publisher. Please include $2.50 shipping & handling for the first book, and 50 cents for each additional book. California residents include local sales tax. Write for our free complete catalogue of over 400 books and tapes.

Ship to:

Name _____

Address _____

City _____ State _____ Zip _____

Phone_____

Celestial Arts

Box 7123

Berkeley, CA 94707

For VISA or Mastercard orders
call (800) 841-BOOK